# 2000 Miles on the Appalachian Trail

## by Donald J. Fortunato

To my father

# TABLE OF CONTENTS

1. What is the Appalachian Trail?..................... 9

2. Preparation for the Long Hike ................... 15

3. Blue Ridge Country ........................... 20

4. Mid-Atlantic and Southern New England States .... 79

5. Upper New England ....... Katahdin Bound...... 107

   References ................................. 156

# CHAPTER ONE

## WHAT IS THE APPALACHIAN TRAIL?

The Appalachian Trail is a continuous marked wilderness foot trail along the crest of the Appalachian Mountain chain from Springer Mountain in Georgia to Mount Katahdin in Maine. In its 2,100 mile length through fourteen states, the Appalachian Trail (AT) leads through some of the finest mountain wilderness to be found in the eastern United States.

Its greatest elevation is 6,643 feet at Clingmans Dome in the Great Smokies. Its lowest elevation is at the Bear Mountain Bridge crossing of the Hudson River. The elevation here is only 115 feet above sea level.

The Appalachian Mountain system is a relatively unbroken range comprised of successive mountain ranges and somewhat parallel ridges. They are separated by longitudinal valleys. The entire range is essentially jumbled. Highway crossings are sometimes used in crossing valleys from one ridge to another.

The Appalachian Trail project has been truly a mammoth recreational endeavor carried out by interested individuals and outdoor groups in cooperation with state and federal agencies. The idea of a seemingly endless "super trail" was conceived by Benton MacKaye of Shirley Center, Massachusetts. MacKaye wrote:

> "The old pioneer opened through the forest a path for the spread of civilization. His work was nobly done and the life of the town and city is in consequence well upon the map throughout the country. Now comes the task of holding this life in check, for it is just as bad to have too much urbanization as too little. America needs her forests and her wild places as much as her cities and sheltered places."

MacKaye presented his plan in an article, "The Appalachian Trail, An Experiment in Regional Planning," in the October, 1921 issue of the Journal of American Institute of Architects. His proposal aroused enthusiasm among outdoor organizations in the Northeast. Clubs in the New York area first embraced the proposal of this new trail.

Under the leadership of Raymond Torrey, the first section of the Trail was completed in the Harriman-Bear Mountain section of Palisades Interstate Park in 1923. The distinctive Appalachian Trail (AT) marker and monogram was designed by a Major William Welch. The New York-New Jersey Trail Conference was formed and the Trail was carried westward toward the Delaware River.

As of 1921, four existing trail systems

could be incorporated into this super trail. The Appalachian Mountain Club maintained trails in New Hampshire. In Vermont, the lower 100 miles of the Long Trail could also be used. The Dartmouth Outing Club was maintaining a trail system in the Green and White Mountains. Finally, trails in the Palisades Interstate Park in New York could be utilized. These four sections however, only totalled 350 miles out of the proposed 2,000 miles.

By 1926, MacKaye's proposal was waning and almost died out until Arthur Perkins of Hartford, Connecticut resurrected the project. Perkins enlisted the aid of Myron Avery of Lubec, Maine. As chairman of the Appalachian Trail Conference from 1931 to 1952, Avery sought the aid of hundreds of people to continue the project.

Many active outdoor and hiking groups have developed along the Trail since that time. Most adopted the name Appalachian Trail Club with the prefix of their particular region (i.e., Maine Appalachian Trail Club).

Much of the Appalachian range in the South was in public ownership, particularly in expansive National Forest lands. The U.S. Forest Service and Civilian Conservation Corps (CCC) marked and cut trails in those areas. Three-sided shelters commonly known as lean-tos were erected. Other outdoor clubs built trails and shelters needed in their respective locales.

The Appalachian Trail was completed in 1937 with the last two miles opened on Mt. Sugarloaf in Maine. Some 60% was in public lands while 40% was on private lands at that time.

The Appalachian Trail Conference (ATC) was formed in 1925 with the Conference headquarters originally in Washington, D.C. The ATC headquarters has since moved to Harpers Ferry, West Virginia.

Courtesy Appalachian Trail Conference

The ATC determined the route and coordinated the work of outdoor organizations to complete the AT. The Conference now functions as a private, nationwide organization in representing citizen interest in the Appalachian Trail and is dedicated to the preservation, maintenance, and enjoyment of the Trail.

Trail mileage within individual states is as indicated below:

## Appalachian Trail Mileage by States

| | | | |
|---|---|---|---|
| Maine ........ | 275 | Pennsylvania .... | 231 |
| New Hampshire | .158 | Maryland ........ | 42 |
| Vermont ....... | 147 | West Virginia ... | 16 |
| Massachusetts . | 89 | Virginia ........ | 528 |
| Connecticut ... | 49 | Tennessee/North | |
| New York ...... | 90 | Carolina ........ | 369 |
| New Jersey .... | 74 | Georgia ......... | 76 |

TOTAL .... 2,144 Miles as of 1991.

On October of 1968, President Johnson signed into law the "National Trails System Act" to provide a nationwide system of trails. The Appalachian Trail and Pacific Crest Trail were the initial components in the system.

The ultimate goal of that Act is to insure an adequate right-of-way for trails so as to provide for the maximum outdoor recreation potential and conservation of significant scenic, natural, historic, and cultural qualities through which the trails pass. The U.S National Park Service and U.S. Forest Service are responsible for protected corridors along the AT in National lands.

An amendment to the National Trails System Act was signed into law by President Carter in March of 1978. This "Appalachian Trail Bill", as it is known, authorizes monies to purchase lands along the Trail.

The National Park Service along with the Forest Service and individual states, under ATC leadership, has since been able to purchase corridors of about 1,000 foot wide where the AT traverses private property. To date, only 75 miles of the Appalachian Trail remain in private ownership.

The Trust for Appalachian Trail Lands has also been instrumental in acquiring and holding desirable tracts of land until federal funds are allocated for purchase. Hopefully, the entire Appalachian Trailway will be protected in the near future.

The Appalachian Trail has been a source of enjoyment to backpackers, day-hikers, fishermen, bird watchers, and many others. It is imperative that we who live in this hurried society have access to wild and scenic places afforded along the Appalachian Trail. For of the Trail it has been written:

> "Remote for detachment, narrow for chosen company, winding for leisure, lonely for contemplation, the Trail leads not merely north and south but upward to the body, mind, and soul of man."

# CHAPTER 2

## PREPARATION FOR THE LONG HIKE

In deciding what equipment to carry along when backpacking the entire Appalachian Trail it must be realized that the choices are largely a matter of personal preference. Veteran hikers are going to tote along in their packs items which, through trial and error, they have found most suitable. One contemplating walking the entire Trail would do well to consult with several long distance hikers to see what their preferences of equipment are.

During the first month of my hike, other through hikers and I weeded out equipment we disliked or felt was too heavy.

My equipment list read:

- Kelty BB-5 Expedition pack & frame
- Sleeping bag (fiberfill or down rated to +10$^{\circ}$F)
- Ensolite pad

- Two-man tent or tarpaulin
- Thirty feet of nylon rope
- One pair light Boy Scout type long pants
- Cutoff shorts, (the more cutoff, the lighter they are)
- Two T-shirts
- One long sleeved, light shirt for camp
- Hiking boots (light or medium weight and well broken in)
- Light sneakers for camp
- Three pairs of inner socks (such as Olefin)
- Three pair wool socks
- Silicone waterproofing
- Two bandanas (serve as handkerchief, potholder, etc.)
- Light rain parka
- Down paraka (for White Mountains and Maine)
- Portable Optimus stove
- One pint fuel container with Coleman fuel
- Disposable lighter
- One cooking pot and plate (Sigg brand is excellent)
- Fork and spoon
- One quart canteen
- 2-1/2 gallon water jug for camp
- Scouring pad
- Soap with container
- Small towel
- Toothbrush and two ounce tube of toothpaste
- Toilet paper
- First aid kit (bandages, aspirin, antibiotic ointment and salt tablets)
- Snake bite kit
- Spare matches in waterproof case
- Small flashlight
  Optional, but nice

16

- 35 mm camera (I carried durable Canon FtB)
- Film and prepaid mailers (sent to town post offices along the Trail)

Food can be planned in two ways: (1) buy freeze-dried food (Mountain House is excellent) or dehydrated food and have it mailed to you along the way or, (2) buy food as you pass through towns. We opted for the latter method for several reasons. First, freeze-dried food can be expensive and you must rely on arriving at the post office during postal hours to pick up your food package. If one gets into a town on Saturday, he must wait over in town until Monday. Second, by purchasing food in the towns you pass through every four or five days, you are assured of wasting little time. I sent freeze-dried food only to the Great Smokies and White Mountains to reduce weight. The kinds of food available throughout the trip are discussed in the succeeding pages.

Fuel, usually in one-quart cans is also easily obtainable in these small towns. Chris Wile, my hiking partner, and I would split a quart of fuel which would last for quite some time.

Travellers checks can be used to buy food and obtain lodging, being redeemable virtually everywhere. I spent approximately $500 during the four month trip, excluding film paid for by my college.

A whole passle of publications are available from the Appalachian Trail Conference. The following are a must:

1. Ten "Guides to the Appalachian Trail," including their respective maps. These books are full of information on detailed trail data in both north/south and south/north directions, sources of water, shelter locations, fire and camping regulations in the guidebook area,

geology and local lore, and much more. We diligently studied these guides before departing on our long trek. Since we began in Georgia, the north/south directions were removed; the guides were mailed to the town just before the beginning of that appropriate guidebook area.

2. Appalachian Trail Data Book

3. The Appalachian Trail, A History and Anthology. In addition, state road maps can be used in conjunction with the guidebooks to easily locate Trail crossings at highways.

Other recommended reading includes:

- Hiking the Appalachian Trail, Rodale Press, Inc., 1976.

- Appalachian Hiker II, Ed Garvey, Appalachian Outfitters, 1978, (with several photos by this author).

- The New Complete Walker, Colin Fletcher, Alfred A. Knopf Publishers, 1977.

In preparing to walk the A.T., I did several things to keep in good physical condition and build endurance. I had been training in Goju-Ryu Karate for sometime previous, and I also ran four miles every night. At best, one should run a few miles at night and hike on weekends prior to setting off for a journey on the A.T. As I have emphasized in the following pages, taking on the task of walking the entire length of the A.T. is not a weekend jaunt through the woods. The strenuousness of the terrain found on the Trail and the rigors of trail life must not be underestimated. Walking the entire A.T. was the MOST physically and mentally grueling task I have ever undertaken in my life.

We chose to begin our hike in Georgia in April, like the majority of hikers, for several reasons. First, there is still plenty of snow in Maine until June; second the mosquitoes, black flies and no-see-ums are a serious problem in Maine and New Hampshire in late spring and early

summer; and third, the tramper starting in the
south to north direction in April follows the
spring season as he/she proceeds north.

Above all else in packing your bags for the
hike on the A.T.--------go light!

## CHAPTER 3

## BLUE RIDGE COUNTRY

As our train rolled through the night, stopping occasionally at some small Southern town to discharge passengers, I pondered the long, interesting hike ahead of me. Thoughts of new places and new experiences rambled through my mind.

The train from Philadelphia, Pennsylvania arrived in Atlanta, Georgia at 10:30 a.m. on April 15, 1974. A bus out of the city brought us to the small town of Jasper, Georgia. Finishing lunch, Art Loder, a college roommate, and I summoned a taxi for $10 each to bring us to the trailhead.

The driver told us about the Georgia mountains in a long, Southern drawl as we raced the last 22 miles toward the Trail. We bid the taxi driver farewell at the 8.8 mile access trail to the A.T. in beautiful Amicalola Falls State Park. Spectacular 500 foot falls cascade down Amicalola Mountain, creating a "silver streak" visible from many highways in the area.

We fitted our awkward packs and began hiking. Our first half-day brought us 5.4 miles to Black Mountain (elev. 3600 feet) over a steep, strenuous trail. We went to sleep...tired. We awoke at 7 a.m., ate breakfast and ascended, then more steeply to Springer Mountain, southern terminus of the Appalachian Trail. Snapping several photographs, we signed the trail register noting quite a few other hikers, too many to count, shared our same dream. It seemed like everyone had written the following: "Georgia - Maine".

During the past several seasons, an estimated 500 hikers annually attempted the 2070 mile trip, while only a mere 10% actually finished in Maine. Since the Trail's completion in 1937 to 1970, only 56 people had walked the length of the A.T. From 1970 to 1978, 400 hikers completed the Trail in a single season. The sharp increase in those attempting to walk the entire Trail can certainly be attributed to the "backpacking fad" in the early 1970s. Every college kid needed a backpack and down jacket and so, the potential number of end-to-enders sky rocketed. We would soon learn that it takes much more than an infatuation with backpacking to complete the Trail.

In Hawk Mountain Lean-to that night, we had met two other through-hikers, Chris Wile of Massachusetts and Bob Ferguson of Louisiana.

My idea to walk the entire Appalachian Trail spawned in high school, having backpacked quite a bit during those years. I read in an Appalachian Trail Conference newsletter an account of a college student who had hiked the length of the A.T. and received college credit. Since I was entering college right after high school and had a desire to hike the Trail, it appeared to be a great idea.

During my freshman year at Stockton State College I started the wheels turning. I arranged

21

to take time off during the spring semester of my junior year. Dr. Gerald Enscoe, Professor of Literature, and I agreed I would prepare a day-to-day journal of my experience along the A.T. Dr. Enscoe did have trouble, though, convincing his Department Chairman that my project would be genuinely worthwhile and that a student can, indeed, learn outside the classroom. Later that summer of 1974, I presented a 90 page typed journal to Dr. Enscoe.

My other independent study was to keep a detailed account of wildlife I would see along the Trail, recording species, physical characteristics, time of sighting, temperature, type of habitat, etc. This project was done under Assistant Professor of Wildlife Biology, Gary Sawhill.

In total, I received eight credits for these two independent studies.

Next morning, April 17, U.S. Army Ranger helicopters practiced take off and landing manuevers in an open field close to the lean-to. We bagan hiking at 9:30 a.m., remembering the guidebook's warning of Ranger booby traps along the Trail.

After a full day, we reached Woody Gap and hitchhiked into Suches, Georgia to get supplies. The conclusion of my daily journal entry for this day read:

> "We are getting accustomed to this way of living-getting up early, eating breakfast and hiking all day. It hurts to push on, but it's worth it. Total--13 miles for this day. We will have to begin hiking earlier, like 6:30 a.m., to bring our daily mileage up to 18 or 20 miles."

The Appalachian Trail in Georgia is almost

Appalachian Trail plaque set in rock

entirely within the 720,000 acre Chattahoochee National Forest, one of the eight National Forests the AT traverses. Like many of the fascinating names along the Trail, Chattahoochee is Cherokee Indian for "flower painted rock."

Following a switchbacked trail, the next day brought us to the summit of Blood Mountain at 4,461 feet. This was the highest point the AT passes in Georgia.

According to Indian legend, so fierce a battle was fought between the Cherokee and Creek Indians that the mountains ran red with blood. The color actually comes from the reddish tint of hardy lichens covering the rocky slopes.

My journal read:

"Views from Blood Mtn. were out-standing. From atop a huge boulder Chris, Art, and I peered out to see many mountain tops. A cool refreshing bleeze blew against our faces after the long climb. We welcomed the silence, soft breeze, and magnificent view that was more than an adequate reward for the work of climbing the mountain."

By this time, our leg and back muscles and feet were in terrible shape, despite any prior conditioning or exercise regiments. Most had numerous blisters, some the size of half dollars and larger! I suffered from heel tendonitis, making it painful to put any weight on my heels.

Upon reaching Neels Gap, we all decided to lay over a few days in Vogel State Park to recover. The limited mileage we could hike was just not worth it. Attempting to hike with sore or blistered feet would be like racing the Indy 500 on flat tires.

We all showered, washed our clothes at the

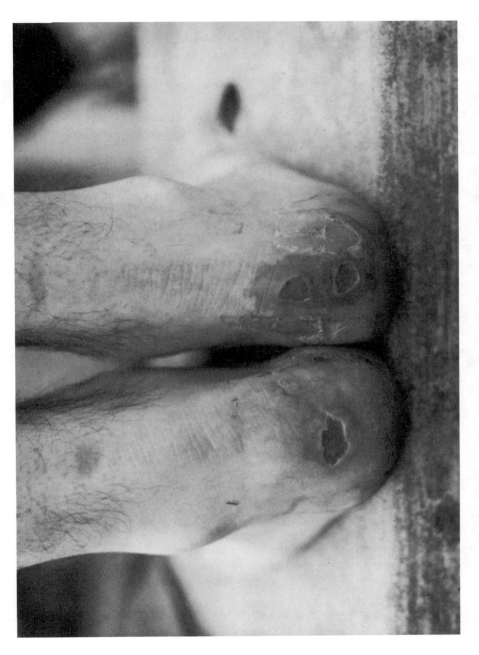

Blistered feet of AT through-hiker

campground laundry, and then lounged around watching the girls. Through-hikers Art Loder, Chris Wile, Marty, Pete and myself were laying over. Several of the guys treated their feet with "Tough Foot", a preparation used to toughen dogs feet!

The geology of the Appalachian Mountain System, with its many component ranges, is quite an interesting story. Long before the Appalachians, there was land and sea. Sediments were laid down in the ancient sea and on land. Former rock material was weathered and transported to a place of accumulation. This weathered material in the form of gravel, silt, sand or clay was transported most often by water in streams, glaciers, or ocean currents. Some material was transported by landslides or wind. These sediments, once deposited, are stratified and solidified to form sedimentary rocks. Sand deposits form sandstone, mud and silts form shale and siltstone, sea shells and the like form limestone, plant deposits form coal, and so forth.

The formation of the Appalachians consists of more than just one episode. The two different sections involved are the northern or New England Appalachians, and the southern Appalachians, basically north and south of New York City, respectively.

In the northern Appalachians, the mountains were lifted to their highest relief before the close of the Paleozoic, approximately 300 million years ago. By the latter part of the Mesozoic (80 million years ago), the peaks had been eroded to an area of low elevations. Then, about 20 million years ago during the latter Cenozoic Era, the northern Appalachians began to rise slowly once again. Those peaks are now the present day Appalachians.

Besides referring to a geologic time scale, it may aid the reader to know that Precambrian means before life, Paleozoic means early life, Mesozoic--mid life, and Cenozoic--recent life.

The southern Appalachian mountains are an area of folded and faulted Paleozoic rocks, although some areas show little sign of any faulting. Folded mountains are those which are buckled up as often seen where highways cut through exposed "wavy" layers of rock. Fault-block mountains are those in which one block of the mountain mass is either thrusted above or dips below the adjacent mountain block. A well known example is evident at 2500 foot Yosemite Falls in Yosemite National Park where a fault has separated two blocks of mountain. The present chain including both northern and southern Appalachians extends from Quebec's Gaspe to northern Georgia. This is a distance of some 1700 miles as the crow flies. One fascinating final point is that weather and erosion have sculpted the present day Appalachians from a mountain chain that was formerly as high as the Rocky Mountains!

After hitching back to the Trail at Neels Gap the following day, Monday, April 22, we hiked along as the skies threatened rain. A very eerie primeval-like feeling prevailed along the mountain summits created by a soft breeze and rolling mist. We camped at a spacious twelve man shelter five miles past Tesnatee Gap. Water was obtained from a stream directly in front of the lean-to. Good water was almost always available at the lean-tos either from springs or surface water; its location was usually indicated by a sign or a note left at the lean-to by some considerate hiker.

Surface water is that water found in streams or ponds fed by overland flow and occasionally, by an underground water source.

Springs and seeps are underground water sources. A spring is a natural outflow of water onto the ground surface, usually from a definite

Through-hikers at camp in Georgia

opening.  A seep is similar to a spring but dif-
fers in that it has no definite opening.  Typi-
cally, water penetrates through the soil further
up the slope and runs laterally on a pan layer or
bedrock, then overflowing onto the ground surface
where that pan or bedrock nears the surface.

In my journal, the Trail in Georgia is described as, for the most part, a 3 - 5 foot wide
Forest Service cut trail, while footing on rocks
can be treacherous.  Other times, the A.T. follows wide logging roads or fire roads.  The Trail
winds up and down (but to the through-hiker, almost always up) the Appalachian Mountain Ridge,
passing through pleasant deciduous forests and
over exposed mountain summits.  The A.T., following the characteristic 2x6 inch white blaze, is
gradual sometimes, but extremely steep on 50-60%
slopes at others.  The first 30 miles seemed the
roughest.  Trail signs indicated distances to
lean-tos, highways in mountain gaps and so on.

The next two days I walked in sneakers to
relieve the pain in my heels.

On a hot Thursday afternoon, April 25, we
arrived at the Georgia-North Carolina border at
Bly Gap.  Our first state and 80 miles behind us.
We now realized what a genuinely strenuous task
we had undertaken.  Many of us would surely never
finish.

Springer Mountain is the apex of the Blue
Ridge Mountains, a component of the Appalachian
Mountain system.  The Blue Ridge forms an enormous oval with the eastern and western rims 100
miles apart at times.  Lofty, traverse ridges,
enclosing a beautiful elevated valley connect the
two master chains which meet once again at
Roanoke, Virginia.

After utilizing a cross range, the
Nantahalas, the A.T. leads from the east rim to
the more loftier western rim at elevations often
greater than 5000 feet.  It then follows that

western rim for some 300 miles to Roanoke. Several rivers break the western range into segments known respectively as; the Cohutta, Ellijay, Frog, Unicoi, Great Smoky, Unaka, Bald, Iron and Stone Mountains. Through the years, the names of these mountain segments have been extremely confused.

We were now in beautiful, remote Nantahala National Forest (452,000 acres), Nantahala being Cherokee for, "land of the noon-day sun".

Friday, April 26, we logged 18.6 miles, traversing enroute, Standing Indian Mountain (elev. 5498 feet) termed the "Grandstand of the Southern Appalachians". Exceptional panoramic views were afforded in every direction! Trees were now in bud and we noted an increasing frequency of wildflowers, especially trilliums and wild daisies.

At Big Spring Lean-to that night were eight through-hikers; Chris, Art, Bob, Pete, Marty and I plus several new faces--Bruce of Macon, Ga. and John of Columbia, South Carolina. For several days to come, all eight of us would begin hiking on our own in the morning, but meet up that night at the next lean-to. We would exchange experiences and gripes, and generally provide each other with the human companionship one craves while in the wilderness for long periods of time.

The guidebooks, although providing essential information concerning shelter locations, water sources, availability of supplies in towns and regional points of interest, do vary in trail descriptions. What one writer considers steep, another may consider moderate; it all becomes confusing and misleading.

Talk among Art, Chris, and I as we hiked together during the day was of ice cream, Bavarian cream donuts, a good shower, family, and especially...females.

My journal reads:

"Breakfast consists of cold cereal (Cheerios are my favorite) with powdered milk and sugar along with hot chocolate Instant Breakfast. For lunch, I have peanut butter crackers and a cheese (Crackerbarrel is good and keeps). Dinners are either tuna or chicken with rice in a sauce of water, powdered milk and flour. Other dinners are Lipton's beef or chicken dinners. Water is the usual drink. I surely miss good food (lasagna, turkey and the like)."

Our tenth day of hiking, April 28, proved to be of interest as we walked the ridge through the last portion of the 54.4 mile section of Nantahala National Forest. Wesser Bald Firetower provided a breathtaking panorama, and later, a switch back trail followed pristine Wesser Creek. Rhododendron, wildflowers, ferns and mosses lined the Trail creating a vegetative paradise.

The last three miles into Wesser, North Carolina were along country roads dotted with small, habitated shacks. Reaching Wesser, we secured a room at a motel adjacent to the Nantahala Outdoor Center on the Nantahala River. It was related to us the next day that the movie, "Deliverance" was filmed on the nearby Chattooga River and that several of the Outdoor Center instructors had done much of the canoe stunt work for the film.

A huge breakfast of pancakes and eggs were served at the Outdoor Center, then afterwards we milled around the outdoor store which offered everything the backpacker could need. Eating a seafood lunch, we resumed hiking. My journal read:

"At 3 p.m. we began one of the two

most difficult sections to be found on the AT, the Stekoah Mountains. This is an understatement! The Trail rises from the 1,650 foot contour at Wesser to Swim Bald at 4,730 feet in only four miles.

"The climbing was extremely brutal; sweat poured off my face as my heart thundered in my chest. The feeling upon reaching the summit after a long drive is gratifying -- the intense effort we've exerted to reach our goal and a strong feeling of accomplishment.

"We are in the Yellow Creek-Wauchecha-Cheoah Range, the link between the Nantahala and Great Smoky Mountains."

That night was one of the two times I was sick on the Trail. My vomiting and diarrhea was most likely caused by the heat, exertion, and seafood dinner. Although still not up to par the next day, I was able to complete 14 rough miles to Cable Gap Lean-to.

We were out of the Stekoahs and heading toward Fontana Village, a resort town near Fontana Lake, on May 1st. I sent postcards and received freeze-dried food, film, and the second AT Guidebook for North Carolina-Tennessee there. Having Mom mail packages to prescribed Trail towns was working out well.

Meeting a Park Service Ranger, we obtained the required back-country permit to camp at the Smoky Mountain shelters. It was wise that Art and I had left our two German Shepherds home since dogs were not allowed on trails in the National Parks.

Chris, Art, and I began hiking again and crossed 480 foot high Fontana Dam, a huge, towering structure impounding the Little Tennessee

River to create 29 mile long Fontana Lake. It is the highest dam in the eastern states and sixth highest in the U.S. Some 5.26 miles brought us to Birch Spring Lean-to, our camp for the night.

Hiking the Appalachian Trail attracts quite a few interesting characters. One 69 year old man was making quite a story of his adventure. It seems he picked cherries in California for three or four years, quit and then headed East with his two dogs and camper. He parked his vehicle at a road in a gap, hiked eight or ten miles north, turned around, and returned to his camper at night. Next day, he would drive north to the next gap repeating the process. He started his trek in 1949 and planned to complete the A.T. in this manner.

Then there were two older women from San Diego attempting to walk the entire Trail to Maine. "Grandma Gatewood" completed the Trail once at the age of 68, again at 69 and yet once again at 77 years of age! Each time walking in sneakers while carrying only bare necessities. Ray Baker, 56 year old retired farmer with a keen sense of the "lay of the land" and a love of the outdoors was yet another completing the A.T.

My journal entry after the first full day in the Great Smokies, noted:

> "One way to describe today--wet and utterly miserable. It rained all night and everything was 'clammy' when we awoke--shoes, socks and T-shirts. Crawling into wet shorts in the morning must be one of the worst aspects of this trip. The only sane way to do it is to hop into them quickly and start walking.
> "Got going at a late 10 a.m. in rain parka and rain cover on pack. Real ominous day--occasional rain and

33

Trail marker in mist at Great Smoky National Park

Chris Wile on graded AT in the Smokies

rolling mist across the peaks. Passed over Gregory Bald, Russell Field, and Spence Field which would not afford fine views this day. Walked 15 miles today with wet feet and in wet clothes.

"I thought of the kind of person it takes to walk the AT in a single season. We suffer with sore feet, sweat like crazy, hike till we are exhausted, and deprive ourselves of all the modern conveniences. It's hard to explain why we go on sometimes; emotional will appears to be the key. Everyone is determined to walk the entire distance.

"Got into Derrick Knob Shelter at 7 p.m. to find through-hiker Marty and six other weekenders. Ate a good supper and ready for bed at this hour of 9:15 p.m."

The following day again was damp and misty. Park Service cut trail led, with constant ascents and descents, along the Smokies, the loftiest and most rugged range in the East with the exception of the Black Mountains of North Carolina.

The beautiful Smokies are high ridges in an incongruous arrangement cut by deep valleys and gorges. The AT follows the central ridge of the Smokies above the 6,000 foot contour in an east to west orientation along the North Carolina-Tennessee border. Other ranges in the Appalachian system generally follow a northeast-southwest direction.

The soils in the Great Smokies along the Appalachian Trail, as indicated in the Soil Conservation Service Cocke County Soil Survey, are mostly "Stony rough land" or "Ashe loam, steep phase." The SCS information shows the bedrock is granite, gneiss, and schist with many outcrops. Where there is some Ashe sandy soil material, bedrock is found at a shallow depth usually not more than one or two feet from the surface. As with many of the steep, mountainous soils found along the Appalachian Trail, its best use is for forest land.

Other portions of the Smokies along the A.T. are underlain by quartzite and slate. Shallow Ramsey soil with 20-70% of the surface exposed to bedrock are found in these areas.

After Double Spring Lean-to, named for its twin springs, we walked through beautiful birch and spruce woods and then among a virgin stand of red spruce and Fraser (balsam) fir. Anakeesta, a name used often in the Smokies, is Indian for "place of balsam".

The vegetation at elevations above 4000 feet is not endemic, except for the Fir, but resembles conditions found a thousand miles to the north in the Aboreal Zone. Climbing 1000 feet in the Smokies is equivalent to traveling 300 miles northward. Apparently, these upland forests are what remained from the Ice Ages that, thousands of years ago, pushed cooler climates and more northerly vegetative species southward.

Annual rainfall in the Smokies averages more than 60 inches in the valley and 85 inches at higher elevations. The excessive moisture conditions spurns lush vegetative growth, often resembling a tropical rainforest. Some 1400 kinds of flowering plants, 350 mosses and liverworts, 230 lichens, and 2000 kinds of fungi exist in the Park. Native trees including magnolia, oaks, mountain silverbell and poplar number some 130 species, more than in all of Europe.

While walking in the Park among huge conifers, moss covered rocks and trees, wildflowers in profusion, and a rolling blue mist (hence the name "Smokies"), we felt like adventurers in a mystical forest in some fairy tale.

Later the same day, we reached Clingman's Dome (6643 feet), highest point on the A.T., named for General Thomas Clingman, explorer of the Carolina Mountains. We camped at Mt. Collins Lean-to. It is interesting that the three-sided shelters in the Park are completely enclosed on the open side by a cage which is to be latched at night. The intent is to keep black bears, attracted by hikers food, out of the shelters at night. There have been several instances of bears damaging tents, packs, and cars attracted by sweet-smelling goodies. The problem could be minimized if tourists would not feed the bears and hikers would keep their backpacks out of reach at night. Other wildlife in the Park include; white-tailed deer, red and gray fox, bobcat, turkey, grouse, wild boar, bald and golden eagle, and more.

Our fourth day, May 4, in the 800 square mile Smokies wilderness brought us past "touristy" Newfound Gap and then Charlies Bunion.

The "Bunion" was enshrouded in fog and we had no idea what a sheer cliff existed to our left. The name of this precipitous feature has an interesting story behind it. It seems that the sheer, northern cliff was forest clad until 1929 when a terrific rain storm swept away much of the soil and vegetation, leaving a bare plug pointing toward the sky. A hiking party intent on seeing the damage included Charlie Connors known for a protruding bunion on one of his hiking feet. Upon seeing the sheer, rocky pinnacle, one member of the party remarked, "That sticks out like Charlie's bunion," and hence, the name.

This same day, I heard the long, melodious call of the winter wren, pausing several times to enjoy its music amidst the mountain silence.

Upon reaching the Big Pigeon River, we left Great Smoky National Park the next day. I felt the Smokies were the most beautiful area along the AT, despite our wet feet and constant "clammy feeling."

It was now Monday, May 6, and Art, Chris, John, and I were in 482,000 acre Pisgah National Forest in the Bald Mountains province. We began at 9 a.m. and ended at Walnut Mountain Lean-to for a long 21 mile day.

We had been steadily increasing our daily mileage from 9-10 miles at the onset of our journey to 18-20 miles at this point. Our physical condition had noticeably improved; our legs were strong and we had lost plenty of weight. Breaking once every few hours, our pace was 2.5-3.5 miles per hour. We moved steadily up ascents without pausing and our breathing was constant and controlled. We agreed that no matter what form of exercise done prior to this trek, we were now in the best condition of our lives.

Backpacking burns up to 1400 calories an hour whereas other strenuous exercise burns only about 800 calories per hour.

A May 7 journal entry read:

"Nice easy walk on a gentle, graded trail through beautiful ridge country on the North Carolina and Tennessee border. The sky was clear and deep blue with the temperature at a balmy 75 degrees. Made 12.6 miles to the town of Hot Springs, N. C. on the French Broad River in 4 1/2 fast hours.

"Bought food, of course, and picked up mail, the lifeline back to home and friends. Checked into Alpine Court Motel; soft bed and full stomach tonight.

"Hot Springs is a small town with a slow pace of life, entirely different from the Northeastern way of life. The people are very friendly especially shop owners who know, of course, how hikers will spend money. Through-hikers will enter a grocery store and obtain the makings for three or four sandwiches washed down with a quart of milk and topped off with some ice cream for dessert.

"Our routine is to get something to eat, read and send mail, buy necessary supplies and perhaps another snack, and then move on. The Trail passes through these small towns every five days or so, or at least reaches a highway where the hiker can travel to a nearby town.

"Looking forward to resting, reading, and generally just taking it easy tomorrow."

On Wednesday, May 8, we rested our exhausted, overworked bodies in Hot Springs. We shopped, wrote postcards, and watched this small, Southern town liesurely move through its daily pace.

The following day we hiked and later camped at Spring Mountain Lean-to. As daylight faded, the through-hikers constant bedtime companion, the lean-to mouse, made mad attempts to get into our packs for food but only to be bombarded by a barrage of sneakers. That night I also heard the eerie, mysterious call of a nearby owl.

For the next several days we traversed game management areas and cattle pastures toward Sam's Gap, end of the Pisgah Forest section.

My journal entry for Saturday, May 11 explained:

Art and Chris at Spring Mountain Lean-to, N.C.

Trail sign at Spivey Gap, Tennessee

"Began at 8:30 a.m. and the day was a strenuous one. Much of the hiking was in cattle pastures and fields. The steep knob walking was tedious with no worthwhile views.
"Although the Appalachian Trail is a crest line trail, I'd suggest it skirt the outside of peaks if there are no views. The crossing and re-crossing of pasture fences was tiresome and trail blazes were bad. Disgusted with the entire day. Total 18.4 miles by 6:30 p.m."

We entered Cherokee National Forest (615,000 acres), the fourth of eight National Forests traversed by the Trail, on our 26th day of hiking. The Pisgah and Cherokee Forests parallel each other up the North Carolina-Tennessee border, the former in North Carolina, the latter in Tennessee.

The National Forests are administered by the U.S.D.A Forest Service, a sister agency to the Soil Conservation Service, of which I was once proudly employed for nine years.

The Forest Service manages these forests on the multiple use principle for sustained yields of timber, water, forage, wildlife, and recreation. Upon walking the Trail, the hiker sees but a small portion of the vast acreage contained within them. The end-to-ender will surely attest though that the Trail seems to be routed over the highest, most rugged peaks in those National Forests.

We crossed Big Bald (5,516 feet) in fog and high wind. The sun finally emerged turning a wet, depressing day into a dry and pleasant one. We set up camp at No Business Lean-to.

To this point, although carrying a tent, we had almost exclusively used the fine system of lean-tos found in the South. They have wooden floors, bunks, and picnic tables to use for cooking and writing. Many of the shelters were designed and built by the Forest Service, while older ones were built by the Civilian Conservation Corps (CCC) in the 1930's. Lean-tos are conveniently spaced on the A.T. to be one days' hiking distance apart.

Next day we got started after a cool night in the 30's. The Trail followed jeep trails and cut-trail along Temple Ridge, at the 3200 foot contour, with inspiring views into the deep Nolichucky River Gorge. We descended by switch-backed trail. Switch backs are utilized on steep slopes to reduce the erosion hazard. The idea being to zig-zag the trail back and forth down the hill every 300 feet or so to reduce the velocity of surface water on these shorter slopes. Gully formation is thereby minimized.

We had now entered the Unaka Mountain province. Unaka is Cherokee for, "land of white mountains", referring to the white quartzite cliffs so typical of these peaks. Geologically, the rocks of the Unaka Mountains are of great age. Iron, manganese, and some silver and gold have been discovered and mined there. The Unaka region also has a rather interesting historical past in that the "Great Indian Warpath Trail", the greatest of all Indian trails, extended along its base. This Indian Trail extended from the Creek territory in Alabama to Pennsylvania, a valley or lowland counterpart of the present day Appalachian Trail.

On May 14th, we reached Hughes Gap (4040 feet) and began the steep ascent of Roan Mountain at 6200 feet, a rise in elevation of 2160 feet in a mere 2.5 miles. The walk, though, was among rhododendron, Fraser fir, and red spruce. Upon arriving at a grassy alcove, to our right was a Forest Service parking area near Roan High Bluff

(6267 feet) and some 1200 acres of rhododendron gardens and open grassy areas. Here in a unique natural garden, Catawba Rhododendron grows in profusion. The purplish-pink flower blooms in the second or third week of June and attracts thousands of spectators and an annual Rhododendron Festival.

Catawba Indian legend explains the existence of this garden as the site of a great battle fought between their people and all other Indian nations of the earth. After many days, the legend states, the Catawbas were victorious but not after much blood had been shed. Ever since, the rhododendrons have bloomed red to pay tribute to their fallen warriors.

We proceeded through more cool firs to Carvers Gap Picnic Area and drank from a fountain whose water was as cold as ice. Crossing paved Roan Mountain Cloudland Road, we ascended grassy Round Bald (5826 feet), Jane Bald (5807 feet), and thence on to Grassy Ridge Lean-to. At 8:10 p.m., after supper Chris, Art and I returned to open Jane Bald to witness a magnificent, colorful sunset. The treeless, grassy summit heralded views in all directions. As always, I recorded these unique events on film.

There are approximately eighty balds occurring between Virginia and Georgia, surely one of the outstanding features of the Southern Appalachians.

The balds are mysterious as to their origin and perpetualism. The adage that where ignorance exists, theories abound, is true for the "balds". The bald summits do not approach tree line because of alpine conditions; treeline here would probably be at 10,000 feet and none of the balds get much over 6500 feet. The soil, from available studies, does not lack any essential nutrients. Tree disease, fire and grazing by livestock may be possible answers. The balds existed

Highlight of the Southern Appalachians, the 'grassy bald'

Sunset at Jane Bald in Roan Cloudland, Tennessee

during Indian history and perhaps they cleared these summits by fire as places of worship. No one quite knows for sure.

The Cherokee Indians had an explanation for the existence of these balds perhaps as good as any. They called the balds, "udawagunda" and believed that hornet-like monsters, "ulagus", once inhabited the balds. These ulagus were thought to swoop down and carry off Indian children. The Indians asked the Great Spirit for help on which he stunned the monsters with lightning. The Cherokees were then able to kill the monsters and hence forth, the Great Spirit decreed that the summits should remain unforested so that the Indians could post sentinels to keep watch for other ulagus.

Walking the A.T. certainly has its interesting natural history and local lore.

Since these balds are treeless, the 2x6 inch white blazes are painted on rock outcroppings or on "cairns", small piles of rocks.

May 15 we hiked across elevated meadows and over Big Yellow and Hump Mountains offering outstanding views. At several points beef cattle had decided they to might like a walk on the A.T. and were reluctant to move out of our way. We kept a very close eye on the bulls. Down slope in the draws, springs used by the cattle were "messed up", the guidebook noted.

A running discussion amongst us was whether going uphill or downhill was easier on the legs and feet. My preference is to go downhill, contrary to everyone elses' viewpoint. They contended that travelling downhill rammed their toes into the front of their boots while leaving the knees weak.

Reaching Route 19-E, we hitched into Elk Park, Tennessee to pick up five much enjoyed letters. It was really nice to hear from my Mom, Dad, sister Rosemary, and friends. A telephone call home to Mom was even nicer.

My journal entry for that night related:

"Art, Chris and I have passed more than 80 through-hikers thus far. Many no longer sign the trail registers Ga. - Me., but instead indicate Ga. - Va. or Ga. - NJ. They have dropped out like flies. Our routine is down pretty well--walking by 7:30 a.m. after cold cereal and powdered milk, hike till 12:30 where we find a nice place for lunch and water, and change socks. Our noon time goodies are carried in the outside pouches of our packs, unless it's too hot. For efficiency, we have separate plastic bags for food and clothes. We then hike again, preferably to a lean-to by 5:30 p.m., eat supper, write in this journal and try to keep up with Karate. Then, it's hit the sack by 9 p.m. and wait for the sun to tell us it's time to start a new day."

An amusing incident happened that same night of May 15 at our camp at an equipment shed at Sunset Orchard (permission required from owner John Morgan). A slight shower was falling so Art took advantage of the situation by taking a bath under the clouds. No sooner had he lathered up with soap then the rain stopped. His only recourse was to rinse off at a spring house with ice cold water down the Trail!

Next day, we followed Walnut Mountain Road through quaint farm valleys with fine views back toward the Roan Mountain area. Wildflowers were out in profusion in meadows we traversed. Later that day, we crossed a log foot bridge across

49

Picturesque farm valley along Walnut Mtn. Road

Laurel Fork Gorge in Tennessee

Laurel Fork and for the next half mile, followed an abandoned railroad bed once used to transport timber out of the Laurel Fork Valley. A steep descent took us to the base of spectacular forty foot Laurel Falls.

Laurel Fork, upon leaving its steep gorge, drains a forested valley of 14,528 acres bounded by White Rocks, Walnut Pond, and South Mountains. An average of 26 million gallons of water a day, is carried over rapids and waterfalls as Laurel Fork twists through a 3-1/2 mile gorge of exceptional scenic beauty. Toward the end of May, rhododendron and mountain laurel abound. A stand of virgin timber remains in the gorge in a steep area above Laurel Falls, so inaccessible, it was passed over when this area was lumbered between 1911-1925. Some 200 million board feet of timber was hauled out of the valley in 80,000 pound flat cars, hauled by 70 ton Shay locomotives.

I missed Art and Chris where I was to turn for Laurel Fork Lean-to, so I proceeded until dusk and camped opposite "Buckled Rock". I had company in my camp, an adopted collie I had fed back at Hump Mountain and had followed us ever since.

At one point during the next several days near Watauga Lake, I had not carried water and walked several hours in hot, humid weather, without reaching any. We were dependent on things the civilized world takes too much for granted, namely: water, sunshine, shelter, and fresh food and fruit. A portion of my diary entry conveys the monotonous, strenuous way of life for the end-to-ender, "Formulated percentage of trail hiking: 50% rocks, stumps, hill climbing, sweat, swearing, and frustration; 20% good times and good views; and 30% sleeping, eating and camp chores."

We all wore shorts as did every through-hiker I came across. Long pants would be too constricting, uncomfortably hot, and would quickly become saturated in a rain or upon brushing against dew-laiden vegetation.

Shortly past Iron Mountain Lean-to, we passed a grave stone bearing the inscription, "Uncle Nick Grindstaff, Born Dec. 26, 1851, Died July 22, 1923, lived alone, suffered alone, died alone." It seems this local character went out West during the Gold Rush era of the late 1800's. He came into a sum of money only to be beaten and robbed. Discouraged and depressed, he returned to his Tennessee mountain home to live alone with his dog, ox, and pet rattlesnake. This story was related to us by a local man who often took orphaned children hiking in the mountains.

On Saturday, May 18 at Abingdon Shelter, a terrific "Southern thunderstorm" struck. The rain pounded against the lean-to roof as lightning flashed and thunder repeatedly cracked closeby. The fury and power of these Southern storms is frightening. At daybreak I thought of our ancestors of 75,000 years ago who, perhaps, sat and peered at the early dawn mist from their shelter as I was.

Our collie companion had left us. Someone suggested he went back to his starting point to team up with a new group of hikers for a free meal.

Sunday, we crossed into our fourth state, Virginia, with 424 miles behind us. Entering Damascus, named after the ancient Syrian capital, we roamed the streets and then checked into the Sportsman Hotel for $2.80 a day. We called home, ate ice cream, and laundered clothes.

Art Loder had decided to end his journey here. He said the grueling, demanding lifestyle of the Trail reminded him too much of the Marines and his days in Vietnam. Chris and I needed no further explanations, but I was saddened to see him leave.

The following day my journal entry declared:

> "Got mail and Southwestern Virginia
> A.T. guidebook and left town at 1
> p.m. Nice walking on graded Forest
> Service trail in Mt. Rogers Recreation Area within Jefferson National
> Forest. The Trail has been relocated, no way to know where the next
> shelter or water may be. Camped near
> stream. Traveled 14.5 miles in about
> six hours--hit the sack early."

The A.T. here was on Iron Mountain ridge
crossing White Top (5520 feet) and Mt. Rogers,
the highest point in Virginia at 5729 feet above
sea level. These two "grassy balds" were covered
with a rolling mist. The crest of Mt. Rogers is
densely forested with red spruce and Fraser fir
reminiscent of the "North Woods" environment.

Further along the Trail, after the quaint
village of Teas, Virginia, we lost the trail
after "mooing" back and forth with a herd of
cattle. Four days out of Damascus, Chris Wile
and I followed the level ridge of Walker Mountain
to Monster Rock Lean-to for a 25.8 mile day. We
were now rising at 6:15 a.m. and hiking an hour
later.

When we arrived at Pearisburg, Virginia a
local radio announcer, Bob White, told us of a
friendly priest who took in A.T. hikers. Bob
gave us a ride to the parish of Father Charles
Beausoleil. My diary relates,

> "Father Charles offered us a place to
> sleep, a meal, shower and the
> luxuries of a television and stereo
> for the mere price of leaving some
> food for future hikers! Certainly a

day to remember. It is this kind of good will and generosity which makes a long, grueling trip like this so worthwhile."

Several other through-hikers were staying at Father Charles', but I doubt if they were going to continue to Maine, like numerous others. We bid Father Charles farewell, and pushed on an uninteresting 20 miles to Bailey Gap Lean-to finally meeting up with 62 year old through-hiker, John Raffo. As many end-to-enders, we always checked the trail registers to see what through-hikers were ahead of us. We had seen John's name and heard stories of this older fellow hiking the entire trail, but could never quite catch up to him. John was accompanied by two other through-hikers, Larry Good and Bob Fine. Chris and I would walk with these three fellows for the next several days.

Other through-hiker acquaintances we walked with in Georgia and Tennessee had fallen behind our pace or dropped out.

Johns Creek and Sinking Creek Valley were especially scenic; flaming azaleas were in bloom everywhere. Trail elevations were at about 3000 - 4000 feet now.

A Tuesday, May 28, 1974 entry noted:

"Steep ascent to Sinking Creek Mountain, then walked along ridge for eight miles on rock slabs in some areas where one wrong move, and it was 1500 feet down! Guidebook says, 'use caution on slanting rocks and ledges, particularly in wet and icy weather.' Really into the routine of hiking from 7 a.m. until noon, breaking for lunch for 45 minutes and cruising till 5 or 6 p.m.

"A lot of the Trail was overgrown and briars often cut our legs; it is a lot of this. It is also banging one's feet on rocks, tripping on roots, and swearing at the never-ending inclines.

"This day we passed farms enveloped in the beauty of the Blue Ridge. Farmers busily worked in their fields making the land their life. We camped under hemlocks near a fine stream. It was a clear day with blue skies. It is this time in camp, a fire brightly burning and stories told by people who walk the many miles of the A.T., that gives walking the Trail its meaning."

Next day, Wednesday, we reached "Dragons Tooth", huge rocks thrust twenty feet in the air, and further along, "Catawba Mountain Top Inn". After lunch, proceeding steeply uphill the Trail emerged from the woods to look over the most spectacular view we had had thus far atop McAfee Knob (3200 feet)! Overhanging rocks jutted out over a forest many feet below. Tinker Ridge was prominent to the east and Catawba Creek Valley below looked like a land-of-make-believe. Houses and roads were mere specs in the vast panorama. Chris and I rested, talking of the extraordinary vista and agreed that nothing could capture our mood. We reluctantly moved on.

Camping near a stream that night we had utilized lean-tos only twice in the last two weeks since they were not at points within our days' travel.

It was interesting to note our lifestyle--we often stopped on the Trail to answer Nature's call needing no tiled bathrooms or silver faucets. One seems to lose the normal inhibitions common in everyday society, truly becoming some wild, often crude "mountain man".

Also interesting to note was the various ways each hiker carried his supplies; some kept their sleeping bags on top in their pack, others on the bottom. One thing agreed by all end-to-enders is to "go light". We carried only bare necessities cutting ounces wherever possible to have a lighter load to carry. My pack usually weighed thirty-five pounds, Chris often carried forty five pounds. All were in outstanding physical shape--strong legs and lean stomachs. Every through-hiker, excepting Chris, lost 10-30 pounds, some more than that in the first two months.

Now five days from Shenandoah National Park, I was anxious to get into New Jersey to go home for a week to see family and take a much needed rest. I reflected in my journal that I was fortunate to have the opportunity to do this sort of trip. My father had to support himself from the age of twelve, having neither a mother nor father. He had to struggle like others of his generation to make a dime. Mom had a family but times were hard; she worked for much of her life for meager wages. Together they were building a future for me so that I could attend college and not struggle with the troubles they experienced in their lifetime.

Descending from Tinker Ridge on Thursday, May 30 after a wet night, we checked into a motel at Cloverdale; John, Bob and Larry got a room next to us.

Laying the contents of our packs on the lawn to dry, we munched on sandwiches and potato salad and drank cold beer.

Bright and early next morning we ate several breakfasts at Hollins Rest and picked up mail. I received another package of several things Mom sent me along the Trail including

2000-milers drying out gear at a Virginia motel

63 year-old John Raffo on the AT in Virginia

Mountain laurel in bloom, Sinking Creek Valley

socks, film and prepaid film mailers. She was
also keeping an assiduous record of my mileage
progress on state road maps. Having someone back
home to mail supplies is a great way to get items
not found in small Trail towns.

The third harmless black snake of our trip
gave us a scare. Nature's camouflage is very
effective on me since I'm color blind. Azaleas
and mountain laurel were in magnificient bloom
all along the AT.

Everyone was quite efficient in camp, going
their own way preparing supper, getting water,
etc. Similar efficiency was common in the morning
break of camp.

We often pondered the kind of tough
challenge we had pitted ourselves against in
hiking the Trail in a single season. We reflected
humbly, though, upon the American Indian who had
neither expensive gear or modern conveniences and
still survived very well for countless years.

The next several days in the Glenwood
District of 610,000 acre Jefferson National
Forest led us through overgrown trails with
intermittent rain showers. Rhododendron enclosed
the AT creating a narrow tunnel at points. The
Trail crossed the famed Blue Ridge Parkway
several times.

A Sunday, June 2 entry related:

> "Another day of rain and the usual
> misery of being saturated. Don't
> really care where we walked, we
> just plodded along. Arrived at
> Matts Creek Lean-to at 4 p.m.,
> washed and the sun finally came
> came out. A 17 mile day and I'm
> disgusted."

Reluctantly, we said our farewells to John,
Larry and Bob at the James River as they headed
into Snowden for supplies. Shortly thereafter

Chris and I got lost near John Styler Hollow Lean-to, as can often happen. The hiker has his eyes fixed on the trail ahead of him and may not look up to see the "double blaze" signifying a change in direction.

Now in the Pedlar District of the vast George Washington National Forest (1,028,000 acres) we stopped for lunch at well constructed Punchbowl Shelter. Twenty four miles behind us we pulled into Brown Mountain Creek Lean-to only to find it filled; camp was made at the Creek itself.

It was June 3, 1974 as we crossed over bald Cole Mountain (4,022 feet) affording spectacular views in every direction. Here we met end-to-ender Charlie Aught of Connecticut and walked with him. The three of us reached The Priest (4063 feet), part of the "Religious Range" including The Friar, The Cardinal, and Little Friar at the 4000 foot contour. Another 22 mile day was ended at The Priest Lean-to. That night, Charlie and I played music, he on the guitar and myself on the harmonica, and, yes, Charlie carried a bulky and heavy guitar. As long distance hikers, we cherished the few hours we could play music and forget the monotony and tedium of walking those relentless miles.

A long descent of 3100 feet in three miles brought us into the Tye River Valley the following day. From the 900 foot contour at the Tye River we climbed to the crest of scenic Three Ridges at 3970 feet. A ledge gave a commanding view back towards the Religious Range and into Tye Valley. Moments like these seemed to justify all the sweat required to reach the summit. Leaving Charlie Aught at Maupin Field Lean-to, Chris and I headed into Waynesboro, Virginia the next day. My ongoing tally of miles completed indicated 765 miles or 37% of the A.T. was behind us.

An excerpt from my journal concerning people at a Howard Johnson's near Waynesboro reflected:

"The tourist bit is hard to relate to, they all seem so impersonal. In camp at night I attempt to find out all about the other hikers staying at the shelter. Perhaps we are starved of human companionship living in the wilderness for so long. Certainly 99% of these tourists could not make the first mile out of the Tye Valley. If one cannot deprive oneself of easy living, one may never know himself."

In Waynesboro, Chris and I checked into a motel, then bought food. The ritual of removing unnecessary packaging from macaroni and cheese, spaghetti and other assorted dinners began. For sometime now, lunch consisted of a sandwich of peanut butter and some variety of jelly removed from their heavy jars and packed into "Gerry tubes". Wyler's lemonade or other drink mixes supplemented lunch and dinner.

Chris needed to get his waterproof boots resoled; he had experienced some trouble with them since they did not breath well in keeping water out. My medium-heavy boots were still in fairly good condition but I planned to replace them at my home with a pair of light work boots fitted with Vibram soles. Along with many other through-hikers I was convinced that medium or heavy hiking boots were a mistake. They felt like lead weights on one's feet and when wet, were twice as bad. If they did become wet, it took several days for them to dry out. Ankle muscles now tremendously strong, did not require the rigid ankle support heavier boots afforded.

"Vibram" lug soles are inherent on any good

63

Appalachian Trail marker and author's Kelty pack

End-to-ender Chris Wile on pontoon bridge

Don Fortunato at Three Ridges Range in Virginia

hiking boot. An Italian, VItale BRAMani, developed this unique sole after a tragic climbing expedition cost the lives of six men. They had all been wearing softer crepe soles when they encountered bad weather and fog. Slippery conditions proved too much for them and they were forced to bivouac for the night. Frostbite and exposure during the night took its toll. Bramani saw the need for a durable sole with good traction for mountain conditions and designed one to fit the need.

We both carried a light pair of track shoes for camp. Nylon inner socks and 60% wool, 40% cotton outer socks proved to my liking.

Laying over in towns for a full day made me restless; presumably our physiological processes were accelerated so greatly from the intensity of the hike that it was difficult to remain relaxed.

Furthermore, the honking of horns and traffic was difficult to deal with since we were accustomed to simple, uncomplicated trail life. Waynesboro was indeed a busy town - shopping malls, restaurants, etc.

Friday, June 7 we hitched a ride back to the A. T. at Rockfish Gap. The Trail crossed several balds used for grazing; stiles and gates were utilized at fence crossings in pastures. Structures of this type were frequently used in pasture areas in the South as well as further north. Since 20% of the A. T. crosses private land, it is imperative that hikers respect landowner rights; simple gestures like closing a gate or not littering can avoid hard feelings with landowners. Too often the Trail has been relocated on roads because of hikers being inconsiderate on private lands.

After 7 miles of hiking, Shenandoah National Park began. The National Park Service claims that due to heavy use, shelters may only be used in the event of emergency or bad weather.

The idea is to disperse campers throughout the Park and away from concentrated use at shelters. As through-hikers, we missed the convenience of using shelters (our home) at night. Permits for backcountry use in the Park are also mandatory.

Shenandoah, the last of two National Parks on the A. T., is some 194,000 acres and graded trails are followed for its 105 mile length. The A. T. parallels the Skyline Drive, crossing it at many points. The area now comprising the Park had been farmed and extensively lumbered years ago. The region prospered from the mid 1700's to late 1800's. Late in the 19th century, economic decline began. Demand for handicraft products dropped off and blight killed most of the chestnut trees. The chestnut was once abundant in the Blue Ridge; its lumber fashioned into furniture while its durability made it ideal for railroad ties, utility poles, and fence posts. A large tanning industry depended on the chestnuts, tannin extracted from its bark and wood. Lastly, nuts from this tree added much to the pioneer meal.

In the early 1900's a Far East fungus entered North America and within a short 50 years, nearly all chestnuts of the Eastern forests were killed. The destruction eliminated more than 9 million acres of the tree. Sprouts from stumps wage a gallant fight for survival, but rarely attain a height of more than several feet before the blight sets in.

Back to Shenandoah though, with the decline of farming and lumbering, the forest once more took over and today nearly the entire tract is wooded. Some 900 kinds of flowering plants are found in the Park today! Wildlife is also particularly abundant including species of white-tailed deer, gray fox, bobcat, black bear and, of course, rabbits and squirrels.

A Saturday, June 8 entry exclaims:

"At Blackrock Gap at 11:45 a.m., saw a white-tailed deer of about eight months jump in front of us and off into the woods about fifty feet to our left. Standing still, Chris coaxed him closer. The deer ventured toward us to within fifteen feet and I snapped pictures. We saw three other deer this day, all very close. Running into quite a number of people marveling at our accomplishment thus far.

"Much of the A.T. in the Park is well graded and cleared, although there are ascents over knobs with no views. The weather has been clear and bright and wildflowers abound. Halfway through the Park, we camped at Big Meadows Campground. We pitched our tent in a well manicured site amongst other tents and trailers. This night a spectacular sunset turned half the sky red. Nature rewards us in many ways for our efforts to walk the Appalachian Mountain range. Mileage: 834.9."

Upon leaving Big Meadows next morning, several large garbage pails had been overturned; our guess - black bears. A sign at the campground warned, "Bear Country - Protect Your Food and Property." The black bear here, as in the Smokies, are protected and accustomed to offers of food, thereby losing their fear of man.

A thought that reappears time after time in my journal was the idea of "doing it", of finishing the job you set out to do for no other reason than to accomplish your selected goal. We had passed many and had seen them give up this journey - we still pushed on. . .

Dawn in the Shenandoah Mountains of Virginia.

Sign at Big Meadows Campground, Shenandoah Park

Four days after Rockfish Gap, we left Shenandoah Park and arrived at Linden, Virginia to pick up mail and the next AT guidebook. We stopped to talk with a Mr. Singleton and asked if we could obtain some water at his home. He invited us in for a Coke and then offered us a home-cooked meal of ham and scalloped potatoes. Other through-hikers had told us of being invited into someone's home for a "real meal"; our time had finally come. Chris and I ate ravenously and finally bid the Singleton family a very appreciative goodbye. I later sent him, and Father Charles, one of my better 8 X 10 inch AT color prints.

Typical Southern friendliness and hospitality had been exemplified in many ways during our trek whether it was a friendly wave from a farmer working his fields, an offer of water, or assistance with directions to a local store.

One story of hospitality on the AT stands out in Chuck Ebersole's 2,000 mile hike. He and his son got into Vandeventer Lean-to in Tennessee to meet Noah Taylor and his sons of Stoney Creek, Tennessee. Taylor had been collecting moss for local nurseries and planned to spend the night at the shelter until a thunderstorm threatened. Noah decided to move to a nearby cabin he knew of. Upon packing in preparation to leave, Noah said to Ebersole, "Hey you fellas, here are some eggs in a sack. I'll set it up here on the ledge for you." "Okay Noah," replied Ebersole, "Thanks alot." Noah then said, "Here's some coffee to go with your eggs". Ebersole replied again, "Thanks Noah." For the following half hour Noah Taylor managed to rummage through his supplies and give the Ebersoles a bit of everything from his food sack. And if that wasn't quite enough, Noah finally split and stacked firewood for the Ebersole's breakfast!

Chris gazes across Shenandoah farm valley

Weverton Cliffs overlook at the Potomac River

The next two days, June 12 and 13, consisted of road walking. At first it may appear to be a relief walking on macadam roads without the worries of wet underbrush, steep grades, or careful attention to a rocky footway, but hard-surfaced roads take their toll on hiking feet. The constant pounding on the hard roadway quickly tires the hiker's feet.

At one point, where the Trail crossed private property via a dirt road, a conspicuous sign warned, "This is not the Appalachian Trail." Feeling unwelcome, we quickly moved through that property.

Another inconvenience of road walking was finding a place to camp. The only shelter may be to hop off the road into a woodlot and hope you won't be accosted by an irate property owner or be disturbed by a local beer party!

On the first night while camping just off Virginia Route 601, apprehensive as we were of our situation, we heard a strange noise. Suddenly, we awoke exactly at twelve midnight to an eerie, high pitched scream, the likes of which I'd never heard. Chris and I discussed at length what we thought the sound was, perhaps a rabbit crying out when attacked by an owl? All sorts of macabre ideas raced through our heads and we never quite fell back to sleep again. A perfect setting for a Steven King novel!

On June 13, we entered West Virginia, finally completing the long 424 mile stretch in Virginia. Now in our fifth state, we arrived in Harpers Ferry, home of the Appalachian Trail Conference. The town is steeped in Civil War history and we explored several of its' sites. Out of Harpers Ferry, the Trail was routed on the towpath of the abandoned Chesapeake and Ohio Canal for a most pleasing and level two miles. A steep ascent, reminding us that we were indeed still on the AT, led up to Weverton Cliffs unfolding an inspiring view north up the Potomac River.

Home distilling became so established in this region during the Prohibition era that a one, Spencer Weaver thought it might be advantageous to organize moonshiners into a syndicate. Weaver offered good wage and fringe benefits. If jailed, a member received his pay in jail and was loaned money to re-establish his still when he was released. He even covered burial costs of slain members and provided the widows with a pension.

The Maryland A.T. Guidebook claims, "But prosperity may have ruined Weaver; he started drinking his product and mild heart attacks followed. One night he backed his auto into the C&O Canal and was found dead."

Chris and I were now in Maryland, our sixth state, atop South Mountain, the northern extension of the Blue Ridge Range, which we would follow into Pennsylvania to the Cumberland Valley. The elevation of South Mountain is between 1000 - 1600 feet above sea level, a considerable drop from the 4000 foot peaks of Virginia and the 5000 - 6000 foot mountains of North Carolina and Tennessee.

This same day, a most unusual instance occurred. At one point, directly ahead of us a woodchuck was scrambling madly around in a circle. Approaching the animal cautiously, we assumed it was sick and, perhaps, rabid. Raising the sole of my boot it nipped at the bottom of my shoe, refusing to move off the trail. The only sensible approach was to use a stick to hold the animal and zip around the side of it. This I did, then threw the stick back to Chris so he could use the same method.

We passed Gathland State Park where a huge monumental arch had been erected by George Townsend to commemorate the efforts of Civil War cor-

76

responders.  Camp that night was at the Crampton
Gap Shelter.

An entry from my journal of Friday, June 14
related a rather unique day:

"Crossed Lambs Knoll (1700 feet), to
our right was a fence enclosed tower,
to our left some weird governmental
installation. A huge cylindrical
tower with several small antenae and
a large unit lay on the ground in
front of this monolith. The entire
installation was fenced in by a high,
barbed wire fence. Then, proceeding
down a fire road, a hen grouse darted
out behind us and passed us with hind
feathers spread, obviously protecting
her young by this diversionary tactic.

"Further on, a Siamese cat walked out
in front of us and up the middle of
the A. T. for some distance, here in
the middle of nowhere!  This day is
certainly bizarre.  Upon reaching
Route 40 we passed old, historic
'South Mountain Dodsen House,' a
place where many past presidents lod-
ged during trips.  This was a major
stage coach route many years ago; it
seems odd as I pass this way years
later.

"Our next point of interest in Washington Monument State Park was a
thirty foot stone structure commem-
orating George Washington.  This was
the first monument erected in the
U.S. for that president.  Passing
through a powerline right-of-way we
found a slip of paper held to a rock.
The note was written  on White House,

77

Washington, DC stationery and read, 'Hikers, this field is covered with blueberries (Vaccinium angustifolium) great to eat - enjoy, Euell Gibbons.' Bizarre note, but we ate blueberries, nonetheless.

"A brief encounter with a billy goat gave Chris and I quite a scare until his charge was abruptly halted by a chain. Then for no apparent reason, we were suddenly struck with a dizzy, light-headed feeling; we stopped and it soon passed.

"Crossing Interstate 70 via a foot bridge with an attached sign reading, 'Appalachian Trail,' we waved wildly at passing cars below and were greeted with a return wave or honk of the horn.

"In Hemlock Hill Lean-to, after rocky trail conditions that really hurts our feet. Sometimes the monotony and long miles of this hike are simply overbearing. Now in camp looking forward to supper and sleep. Another 20 mile day behind us and tomorrow we cross into Pennsylvania."

# CHAPTER 4

## MID-ATLANTIC AND SOUTHERN
## NEW ENGLAND STATES

Entering Pennsylvania, quite a number of
hikers passed us, in the opposite direction, and
were amazed by our trek. They must have thought
us mad, our pace almost a jog with full packs,
tattered clothes, and that determined thru-hiker
gaze. End-to-enders move and act "like they have
a purpose." We passed a marker for the
Mason-Dixon line established in 1765, and then
entered delightful Michaux State Forest. The
Trail followed South Mountain on the Blue Ridge
chain. Arriving at Tumbling Run Shelter, we
decided to end a 16.3 mile day at a stream that
invited us to take a much needed bath. At the
lean-to a woman with a group of girl scouts gave
us hot dogs, cookies, and drinks they had left
over.

We had not utilized many of the wild, edible
plants located along the AT, excepting blueberries and ramps, a wild native onion to the
Southern mountains. In Virginia, excited with

the idea of a new, wild food to put in our dinner, we cooked seven or eight of the little onions into our meal. For those familiar, only one or two ramps are needed to spice up a meal, and, you guessed it, that dinner was just a bit too oniony!

Other plants along the trail that are tasty include: wild ground and branch lettuce, young watercress found near spring water, teas from peppermint and spearmint plants, and mushrooms, among others. Extreme caution is needed in picking edible mushrooms - the amonita strain is quite deadly.

Many good books are out on edible, wild plants if one is so inclined.

Another Sunday of rain began our day of hiking passing Caledonia Iron Works in Caledonia State Park enroute. The ruins of the furnace built in 1837 by Thaddeus Stevens, a great abolishionist, lay nearby. These iron works operating during the Civil War period were later destroyed by Confederate Troops enroute to the Battle of Gettysburg in 1863. Further on, we passed the former home of the Ege family, now a Potomac Appalachian Trail Club (PATC) shelter. A furnace, forge, coal house, workmen shops, thirty log dwellings, and grist and sawmills were once part of the Caledonia Iron Works complex. Charcoal to fuel the furnaces was produced in flat charcoal heaths, 30 - 50 foot in diameter, still visible along the A. T. in this area.

Two young girls, walking from Maryland to their home in New Hampshire via the A. T. were our neighbors at Tagg Run Shelters that night. It was their seventh day out and they had the usual long distance hiker aches and pains. My hopes for some female companionship were fruitless since they were so exhausted.

The Tagg Run twin shelters for 2 - 3 people each were in terrible condition - the area littered, shelters barely habitable, and the water from Tagg Run undrinkable. These were the first shelters encountered in such awful shape.

The following 12 miles on Monday were uninteresting except for the crossing of the half way point of the Appalachian Trail, approximately 1025 miles from Georgia. Further along we left the Blue Ridge Mountains to cross the ten mile wide Cumberland Valley on hard surfaced roads amidst beautiful farm country. In Allen, Pennsylvania, a horse drawn buggy driven by an Amish gent passed through the middle of town; quite a site in this modern age. Crossing the Susquehanna River, we ascended Blue Mountain, a narrow crest of the Alleghany Mountains leading 142 miles north into New Jersey. This same Blue Mountain peak bears the name, Kittatinny in New Jersey. Much of the land along Blue Mountain is state owned game land.

All through the South, hikers had warned us of the infamous "rocks" of Pennsylvania. These words proved true; the constant pounding of our feet on rocks for 20 - 25 miles a day was quite painful.

On arriving at Route 325, St. Anthony's Wilderness lay before us. It was getting late, about 8:15 p.m. when, through the corner of my eye, I saw a movement to my right, Chris yelled, "Whoa!" I froze turning around to see our first poisonous snake, a 36-inch long copperhead. It lay there in a S shape with head propped up in striking position. We played with it for a while, with a long stick of course, but it never made any aggressive move. It then slowly crawled off.

This snake with its distinctive hourglass markings and copper head, is one of the two poisonous snakes found along the A. T., the timber rattlesnake is the other. The fear of these cold-blooded reptiles is overly exagger-

81

The "infamous rocks" of Pennsylvania

Poisonous copperhead on AT in Pennsylvania

ated. They are terrified of humans and will strike only when threatened, like any animal when cornered. Nevertheless, the wise tramper must be wary when crossing logs, or climbing among rocks and ledges where the snake seeks refuge. Being cold-blooded, they may be seen basking on rocks in 70 - 75 degree weather. These snakes also fill an important niche in the natural realm preying on mice and other small rodents. To kill snakes is cruel, senseless, ignorant to the ways of Nature, and usually is against the law.

The A.T. is the snakes' home so a good snake bite kit should always be carried along with knowledge of how to use it.

The remaining 14 miles in St. Anthony's Wilderness followed abandoned stage coach roads offering a pleasant walk. During the 1800's, this area was the site of a flourishing coal industry with coal mines present throughout.

Reaching Swatara Gap, we stopped at Lauschs' General Store for a bountiful snack. My journal relates,

> "Met Red Egress, local beer and soda distributor, who gave us a bottle of Coke, a dozen eggs, carrots, and lettuce. He has a heart of gold. It is this kind of hospitality and friendliness which adds to the character of the Appalachian Trail journey. It is more than just a hike, it is an encounter with people and places; experiences I will never forget . . . a long 26 miles today."

Proceeding swiftly along Blue Mountain, good views normally afforded at the Pinnacle, Bake Oven Knob, and Wolf Rocks were covered in a humid haze. We knew in just a few days we would get a week long break in New Jersey at my parents home from the rigors of trail life. The Pennsylvania "rocks" seldom ceased.

One of the many saddening stories of how the white man swindled the Indian out of their native land involves the Pennsylvania "Walking Purchase" of 1737. Settlers pushing further into Indian territory thought of a novel idea to decide territorial limits. The Delaware Indians agreed the settlers could receive land measured "as far as a man walks in a day and a half," but the settlers translated this into "as far as a man can possibly walk in a day and a half."

The Pennsylvania A.T. guide relates a line was then drawn straight to the Delaware River. Instead of using only one man, the white men used three, and instead of walking, almost ran covering 61 1/4 miles from the starting point at Washington's Crossing, Pennsylvania. Thereby, they more than doubled the acreage the Indians had expected to grant them. The Indians accused the white man of dishonesty and trickery and aroused a bitter hatred toward the white man that persisted for many years.

We found it difficult to sleep the night of June 23 at Kirkridge Lean-to with the excitement of going home the next day.

Although the sun shone the following morning, the underbrush was wet and we became completely saturated. Thickening clouds and a slight drizzle had begun to fall prohibiting views into the Delaware River from Mt. Minsi.

The Delaware Water Gap dips down almost 1000 feet from Mt. Minsi on the Pennsylvania side, and Mt. Tammany on the New Jersey side. The Gap was formed millions of years ago when great tectonic pressures caused the conglomerate sandstone ridge to rise. The Delaware River eroded the less resistant shale bedrock as the main ridge slowly rose, thus forming the deep water gap found today.

Arriving at National Park Service Kittatinny Point Visitors Center, I marveled at the fact that we had come 1184 miles through seven states. More significantly perhaps was the fact we were 2 out of possibly only 60 through hikers still left on the A.T. What had happened to the 600 or so people who had left Springer Mountain intending to get to Maine in one season? Too much work, I guessed!

Hitching on Interstate Highway 80 and 287 to within 7 1/2 miles of my home, people stared at us in dirty shorts and full packs, perhaps wondering what the hell we were doing!

We surprised my mother by a day and a half and it was wonderful to see her again. Seeing my entire family felt good as we had much to talk about. My German Shephard, Cisco, would not leave my side for several hours. That night at dinner, Chris and I alone all but devoured a whole ham, loaf of bread and a gallon of fresh milk.

Monday, June 24, I wrote some general impressions in my journal:

"Yet another six days left to our stay. We have an entirely different routine here. We don't wake in the mornings to face 20 - 25 trail miles by 6 p.m. that night. We are eating well as Mom is a great cook. Resting well and slowing these muscles down was imperative, as well as the psychological break from a tedious routine. We were 'wound up', pushing the extraordinary avenue of 20 - 25 miles daily for the past eight weeks - a grueling pace, walking ten hours a day, seven days a week! We had long ago become frustrated with trivial things like strings on our tent, our boots, and each other.

"Surely to a normal person, reserved and collected, our eccentricities must have appeared ludicrous. I do miss the Trail though. People in civilized society seem to have a lot of bad habits and often don't know themselves. In the wilderness, there is simply no fooling around. You a-wake to eat breakfast for energy or you can't walk a mile. You get wet, feel miserable and the next minute the sun shines making you feel like a new person. The wonders of the natural realm are all around you; a blossoming flower, a bird's song, or a brook tumbling over rocks so old the human mind cannot conceive the time that has passed. Nature is also harsh. Animals struggle for survival everyday, we walk among jagged rocks where one slip could result in a bro-ken bone. If you can't get help you can die as easily as the squirrel or deer. This is reality, this, is truly life.

"Chris and I glance around wondering which people would have the physical and mental stamina to make this trip; few we conclude.

"I'm extremely anxious to complete the length of the Appalachian Trail. It will be a great moment to reach Katahdin. I have great respect for all trampers, present, past and fu-ture who show the strength, courage and perserverance to complete the 2050 mile walk. We are all a dif-ferent breed. Those who climb Ever-est feel it, those who sail long journeys on the sea feel it; I am proud to be one of this select group.

"My journey has taught me that nothing is impossible. Our experiences thus far have been good and have been bad. It is pure hell to walk over jagged rocks piercing your soles mile after endless mile, or slosh through water, or walk in extreme heat and humidity. But it is also ecstacy to hike amidst a beautiful woodland, in a moss covered ravine, or to reach a mountain summit that has made you sweat to view its' majestic panorama. This is the Appalachian Trail; as life is both good and bad, it is the same.

"We soon leave on the second leg of our trek to Trails' end...Katahdin."

It was now Saturday, June 29 and after reluctant farewells to my family, Chris and I were once more on the Appalachian Trail. Hiking again with a full pack felt very awkward. The Trail followed the long crest of Kittatinny Mountain, an area I have frequented many times. Kittatinny means "greatest hill", according to the Lenni-Lenape Indians, "the original people", who once lived in this region.

This is the same conglomerate sandstone ridge continuing southward into Pennsylvania for 142 miles to the Susquehanna River, bearing the name Blue Mountain on the AT. Northward, within the Ridge and Valley Physiographic Province of New Jersey, it continues into New York and becomes Shawangunk Mountain (aka-the gunks). Less resistant shale and limestone comprise nearby eroded valleys.

The predominant soil found atop Kittatinny Mountain on the AT is Rock outcrop-Oquaga association. Bedrock outcrop occurs on 40-60%

of the area's surface. The Oquaga gravelly loam soil is less than 10 inches deep. Cracks and crevices in the sandstone bedrock is filled with soil material supporting tree and shrub growth.

The U. S. D. A. Soil Conservation Service Soil Survey for this area indicates its best use is for forest and wildlife land.

The A.T. passes beautiful Dunnfield Gorge to glacial Sunfish Pond by a rough, rocky footway. Many ponds were to be passed from here to Maine.

Shortly after Sunfish Pond, the A.T. enters Delaware Water Gap National Recreation Area and keeps within its boundaries for twenty miles to Stokes State Forest.

Mt. Mohican (1500 feet) afforded a fine view down to the Delaware River and the Poconos beyond. Further on, Catfish Fire Tower was passed and then a blue-blazed side trail descended 1000 feet to spectacular Buttermilk Falls, a trip well worth the effort. The A.T. then entered Stokes Forest and ascended the open summit of Rattlesnake Mountain at 1492 feet with inspiring views.

We then reached Route 206 at Culvers Gap and three miles later, Gren Anderson Lean-to to find through-hiker Charlie Aught. We had walked with him further south around Three Ridges, Virginia. It was good seeing him again. Walking alone as Charlie was doing has its advantages and disadvantages. He could hike at his own pace and be alone on the Trail plus not worry about a compatible partner. But if he were to break a leg or be bitten by a snake, a partner could be a life-saver. Also, being alone in the wilderness away from human contact can be lonely. As it is with choice of equipment, it is a matter of personal preference to walk alone or not.

Another Sunday night of rain, common for the past several weeks, left the trail wet next

89

Chris Wile eating at camp

Author looks up the Delaware from Mt. Mohican, N.J.

Mushrooms under pine tree on the AT

morning.

July 1, the three of us reached Sunrise Mountain (elev. 1653 feet) offering outstanding views of the farm valley to the east and wooded region to the west. During autumn, a considerable hawk migration attracts scores of bird watchers to this area.

Losing the Trail twice after Sunrise Mountain because of poor blazing, we crossed Route 23 in High Point State Park. We travelled then five miles on macadam roads to Unionville, New York where we ate and had a few beers. Camp was made further on at Pochuck Mountain, the Indians "retreat place." A tranquil sunset helped us forget a day of hiking on paved and unimproved roads.

Next day and seven _more_ miles of road walking in hot, humid weather left us fatigued and drained of energy. Charlie, Chris and I took a nap at midday to get relief from the heat. Mosquitoes were out in droves but Mom's 6-12 stick insect repellent worked well. We crossed back into New Jersey entering Wawayanda State Park. Wawayanda is a name given by the Lenape Indians to a creek they called "water on the mountain."

The A.T. traverses the breadth of this 10,000 acre Park through upland deciduous forest with intermittent red spruce, white cedar, hemlock, and rhododendron.

We were in the Jersey Highlands Physiographic Province. Hills mostly of resistant gneiss, granite, and schist alternating with valleys of less resistant slate and marble make up this region. For a billion years, between 1-1/2 to 1/2 billion years ago, eastern North America was subject to an episode of deformation. Deep below the surface of the earth, magma invaded the metamorphic basement creating granitoid rock. Magma-invaded crust was then thrust into 10,000 foot high mountains. Over millions of years, erosion

93

wore down these once high peaks (as high as the present day Rocky Mountains) to its basic igneous core today. These rock formations are the oldest in the country, dating back to the Precambrian.

Upon reaching Warwick Turnpike (Moe Road) 700 feet to the right, we bought fresh vegetables and fruits at Moe Mountain Stand. Being on the Trail with a constant diet of instant dinners, we craved fresh food, especially fruit. We camped a little further on.

The next several days were hot with excessive humidity. Haze made views from the open ledges of Bellvale Mountain toward Greenwood Lake not worth the effort. Several ponds invited us to a refreshing swim.

We entered Bear Mountain - Harriman State Park in New York on a hot, humid July 3rd. One enters the Park upon descending "Agony Grind," a 600 foot drop in .33 miles and crossing the New York Thruway. Passing cautiously past several deer along the park road, we were then on the first six mile section of the A.T. This stretch was officially opened on October 7, 1923!

Scrambling over the steep, rocky slope of Green Pond Mountain, we reached pretty Island Pond at 10:15 a.m. and were swimming in short order. The A.T. proceeded up the rocky Island Pond Mountain and through a narrow passage of boulders known as the "Lemon Squeezer." Further along, we passed Three Point Rock, a huge boulder curiously propped up by glacial action.

Reaching Lake Tiorati, we were stunned by the thousands of people - could this be the Appalachian Trail, our wilderness passage? Being accustomed to stopping on the trail to talk with others, no one here even said hello. We ate hamburgers at a refreshment stand and pushed over Bear Mountain (1305 feet) in miserable heat.

Again we ran into crowds of people as we passed Bear Mountain Trailside Museum and Nature

Center where a section of the A.T. was paved! Here also was the lowest point found on the A.T., 115 feet above sea level. A ten cent pedestrian toll was levied at the Bear Mountain Bridge crossing of the Hudson River.

Up steep Anthony's Nose where camp was made, we left the hordes of people far behind. In the vicinity lay abandoned mine shafts of Manitou Mine where iron ore was once extracted for the Revolutionary War effort. Two forts, Clinton and Montgomery, were built on each side of where the Bear Mountain Bridge now stands. In 1777 a chain was stretched across the width of the Hudson to prevent British entry to West Point. However, the British overpowered the Orange County Militia which held these forts and broke the chain.

Friday, July 5, 1974 was a less hot day of about 75 degrees. The Trail was routed on paved and unpaved roads to Fahnestock State Park, when the rains began. I have hiked in Fahnestock at other times and it's a pleasant walk on wood roads, cut trail, and old bridal paths. Stone walls and abandoned stone farm buildings are passed enroute. Mountain laurel is out in profusion in spring time. The grassy wood roads remind one of Harriman State Park and St. Anthonys Wilderness.

My journal that night reiterated a strong theme prevalent throughout its length:

"2 p.m. the rain began, getting us entirely soaked (nothing stops us). About 700 miles to Katahdin. This trip is a compromise - Nature gives us a good view from an open mountain summit or a walk through a moss covered gorge, but we pay the price in rain, rocks, and mud. It is honest out here, the A.T. seems to be our

95

whole existence and the only conceivable future we know, it is the only life we know. The demands of Trail life are demanding . . . hell it's easy to run home, as many have done. But Katahdin is a goal, getting closer everyday. If one cannot pit himself against challenges and win, he is less then he should be."

Now on July 6, the A.T. was routed on a most uninviting twenty miles of paved and dirt roads. A hot shower at Pawlins Park relieved our frustrations somewhat. Chris and Charlie explored the idea of playing ping-pong to break a new world's record in time played; after the A.T. expedition, nothing seemed impossible.

Next day, we entered Connecticut, our tenth state and 1330.49 miles from Springer Mountain, Georgia and 710 miles to Trails end. The New York-Connecticut line is reached at Schaghticoke Mountain, Indian for "land where two streams meet" referring to the confluence of the Housatonic and Ten Mile Rivers at Bulls Bridge. Chris, Charlie and I joyfully crossed yet another state line and hiked .43 miles to the junction of the A.T. and blue-blazed Schaghticoke Mountain Trail. Interested in seeing an old Indian graveyard site, we followed the latter trail .62 miles down Schaghticoke to River Road.

Enroute to the three mile walk into Kent, Connecticut, we passed Schaghticoke Reservation Indian Burial Grounds. Sachem Gideon Mawee established the tribe in this vicinity about 1730. One grave read, "Eunice Mawee, Indian Christian Princess, 1756-1830, the granddaughter of Gideon Mawee."

Arriving in Kent, we decided to lounge around for the remainder of the Sunday in a large, commons area opposite the town post of-

Through-hikers (l to r) Charlie, Chris, and author
clowning around in camp

fice.  Route 7, the main road through town, was heavily travelled.  We enjoyed observing people as they rode by.

Charlie was a lean, interesting character adept at many things.  He entertained us with a juggling act using three pair of socks!  We visited a small grocery store several times during the afternoon in an attempt to curb our insatiable appetites.

Near 7 p.m., a local character by the name of Tom Casey, amused us immensely with his comments.  He nicknamed me, "Karate."  We talked with him for hours.  As nightfall came, we agreed to sleep in a town graveyard, but Chris was a bit apprehensive about this choice of campsite.  Insisting we move, we found a church parking lot to bed down in.

Chris and I bid farewell to Charlie Aught, who wanted to leave the A.T. for a break to visit some family in Connecticut.  We wouldn't meet up with him again for the remainder of the journey. Having received mail, along with the A.T. guide to Massachusetts and Connecticut, we moved north once more.

The Trail was routed in a circuitous manner to take the tramper through Macedonia Brook State Park, at one point, crossing Cobble Mountain (1380 feet) affording good views west to the Catskills and northwest to the Taconics.  Coming off steep, rough Seneca Ledges, the A.T. then followed old River Road along the west bank of the scenic Housatonic River for five miles.  The footway here was excellent, and level!

Reaching Cornwall Bridge at the junction of Routes 4 and 7, I picked up a local newspaper to find out what was going on in the civilized world.  History was being created as the Watergate scandal developed.  The A.T. then ascended through scenic Dark Entry Ravine, an area of hemlocks, waterfalls and tranquil pools.  A short

98

section of paved road past peaceful farms followed and then cut trail led one-half mile through
Cathedral Pines. This extraordinary stand of
white pines reaches 150 feet to the sky with cir-
cumferences so great that two people cannot wrap
arms around a tree and touch each others finger-
tips! The hiker feels as if he is in some dimly
lit, primeval fairy land. One is awed by the im-
mensity of these native conifers and wanders
amidst them with head pointed toward the sky str-
aining to see the tops of these great trees.
Fortunately, this tract is owned by the Nature
Conservacy to be preserved in its natural condition forever.

The Trail continued on, crossing several
ski trails in Mohawk Mountain ski complex. The
A. T. traverses the north slope of Mohawk Mountain within Mohawk State Forest. According to
local legend, the mountain received its name from
a beacon lit by the Schaghticoke Indians to warn
the approach of Mohawks raiding the region exact-
ing tribute.

A small picnic area was reached with excellent pumped, well water before we crossed Route 4
at Bunker Hill.

Chris and I were delighted to be in the
North Woods environment; cool, dark coniferous
forests interspersed with birch.

Before arriving at Salisbury, Connecticut
we passed beautifully forested Deans Ravine, and
then ascended and descended steeply over rough
Barrack Mountain. We set up camp shortly after
this peak.

Next day, July 9, we eventually got into
the quaint New England town of Salisbury where we
obtained supplies before moving on.

Chris and I were now beginning one of my
favorite sections of the A. T., the 16.8 miles
from Salisbury to Jug End. This stretch crosses
Lions Head and Bear Mountain in Connecticut and

Mounts Race, Everett, and Bushnell in Massachusetts. It was in Salisbury in 1971 that three high school friends and I ended a two week hike from Mount Greylock to Salisbury on the Appalachian Trail. My idea to through-hike the Trail in a single season while in college crystallized during this earlier hike. I had some idea during this 1971 hike of how difficult long distance hiking can be.

The Appalachian Trail has always been very special to me and during twenty one years of hiking, I have logged an additional 500 miles on the AT.

Leaving Salisbury, we ascended steadily through forest and pasture land. Farmers usually devote their steeper, stonier, and poorer soils to pasture land.

Enroute we observed interesting glacial kettles. During the Pliestocene epoch, glacial melt water carried large amounts of sand, gravel, and rockflour. Much of this material was deposited in downslope valleys away from the head of the glacier as alluvial fans. The coalescing alluvial fans of many streams from the glacier formed outwash plains. Some of these outwash plains are dotted with undrained holes, most less than 100 feet in diameter.

These holes or "kettles", are areas where a block of ice, stranded during glacial retreat, was buried by outwash gravel. The melting of these blocks of ice left the depressions we see today.

We reached the height of the Taconic Mountains at Lions Head (elev. 1,783 feet) and enjoyed striking views.

A high school group was being instructed in backpacking, map reading, and other various outdoor skills. We stopped to talk to a young man leading the group who was very interested and enthused with our trek, and, of course, we were

Race Brook Falls on AT side trail in Massachusetts

always willing to inform others of our adventures. After our talk, he insisted on lifting our packs to our backs, a gesture of respect we much appreciated.

From here the A.T. turned north and followed the Mt. Riga coal road. This region was once the center of a flourishing charcoal and iron industry. Several miles west was Forge Road, the seat of an essential iron industry, where the anchors of the frigate Constitution were forged.

In a hot 95 - 100 degree sun, Chris and I ascended a long, open slope to Bear Mountain (2316 feet), the highest point in Connecticut. Climbing a forty foot stone monument offered a commanding, although hazy, view of the Housatonic Valley to the east and south; Berkshires to the north; and New York's Catskills to the west. The A. T. Guidebook informed, "note mountain ash and bunchberry, plants of the North high country."

A steep, rocky descent brought us into Sages Ravine. Just ahead of us was an obviously well seasoned hiker moving at a fast rate. He was no match for our physical conditioning though and in short order we caught up with him. He was an A. T. C. member and we stopped to chat. He had walked quite a bit of the Trail and told us what to expect in Vermont and Maine. He also insisted on lifting our load to our backs.

For the remainder of this Tuesday, my diary noted:

> "Out of Sages Ravine and into Massachusetts, our eleventh state. Climbing to the top of Mt. Race, we took a red-blazed side trail to Race Brook Falls. They are a series of five beautiful waterfalls one over 100 feet high, cascading down through a mossy, steep ravine. The area is

incredibly scenic and only a mile off a Massachusetts highway. It is a steep, slippery climb into the waterfalls from that road on a poorly marked trailed.

"After a nice, but chilly, bath I took many photographs using Kodachrome II and a light weight tripod I picked up in New Jersey during our break. The use of the tripod allows me to use slower shutter speeds of 1/2 or 1 second with slow speed film resulting in better color saturation and sharper prints.

"The bugs are bad so I think I'll turn in."

Wednesday, July 10, was a humid day. Now in the Berkshire Mountains of Massachusetts, we passed Mt. Everett and a gem of a lake, Guilder Pond. Descending the steep cliffs of Jug End, one comes to a small picnic area and an excellent piped spring. Each time I have hiked this section from Jug End to Salisbury, Conn., the pipe has always flowed full with icy cold water.

Next came the crossing of the Housatonic Valley - via secondary roads for 6.2 miles, and thence East Mountain State Forest and Butternut Basin Ski Area. Further on in Beartown State Forest we passed another picturesque North woods lake, Benedict Pond.

Next day we arrived at Jacobs Ladder Highway. My diary noted:

"Passing through towns and seeing folks seems odd. We walk out of the mountains where life is simple. We walk, eat, and sleep. The light and weather govern our day, and often our mood. Mans' complex social organization does not pertain to us. Nevertheless, going into a town we know we must abide by those social rules. We cannot relieve ourselves when the urge beckons, nor can we walk about nude, or swear violently over trivial upsets. I believe we are justified in swearing vigorously in the woods to vent our frustrations; our repertoire of choice words is large. The physical and psychological strain of this A. T. marathon demands we 'let off steam.'

"The way of the woods and the way of human society are indeed, two very different things. A person lacks a basic understanding of life if he does not pit himself against Nature and its elements.

"It is a fine day - blue sky and lowered humidity. It's curious to look back over the flowery philosophies I wrote at the beginning of this journal. Those words resemble the 'pretty picture books' written on the A. T. Sure, the scenery is often breathtaking, but the task of completing this trek is long and arduous. After the first 200 or 300 miles you realize the difficulties of long distance hiking; Maine becomes a goal to achieve.

"It isn't going to be exclusively five months of waterfalls, deer gamboling in full view, or effortless walking over gently rolling terrain. This damned job requires toughness and tenacity. You have to keep plodding along, mile after mile, through mud and rocks until you finish what

104

you set out to do.
"Time and Nature have built these mountains, unfortunately, hikers were not considered at the time."

Entering October Mountain Forest (14,189 acres) we passed Becket Mountain (elev. 2178 feet), Finerty Pond, and Bald Top Mountain (2040 feet).

By and by, we reached Cheshire, Massachusetts where a monument paid tribute to a 1235 pound Cheshire Cheese. This piece of cheese, enough to make any lean-to mouse happy, was one days product of the towns' dairies in 1801. It was hauled to Washington, D.C. and delivered to President Jefferson.

On July 12, we entered the Greylock Reservation ascending the semi-grassy bald of Jones Nose on a cool, breezy morning.

Passing among spruce and balsam woods similar to the Great Smokies region, we moved on to the summit of Mt. Greylock at 3491 feet, the highest elevation in Massachusetts. Striking views to the north were impressive. The name "Greylock" dates back to 1817, deriving its name from its "hoary aspect of winter."

We ate a second breakfast at Bascom Lodge and talked with two fellows who had just been on the A. T. in Maine. I had asked them about that state, ever curious of what was ahead of us on the Trail.

A John Denver song on the radio, "Good to be Back Home," made me think of home and the transient existence of the A. T. through-hiker.

Hiking amongst a fine stand of spruce we left the Greylock Reservation reaching Blackington, Massachusetts. Chris and I replenished supplies, picked up the Vermont-New Hampshire A. T. Guidebook, and partook in yet another snack. Camp was established at a small stream a mile or

105

so out of town in Clarksburg State Forest.

# CHAPTER 5

## UPPER NEW ENGLAND . . . KATAHDIN BOUND

Beginning early next morning, we climbed to Eph's Lookout (2254 feet) for a splendid view back toward Greylock and the Taconics. A dense, unmoving mist enveloped the valley below.

Vermont', our twelfth state and 1473.11 miles from Georgia, was under our boots. The Appalachian Trail and the famed Long Trail were now one. The Long Trail is a 260 mile path leading from the Massachusetts - Vermont line along the main ridge of the Green Mountains to the Canadian border. The A.T. turns east off the Long Trail in 94 miles at Sherburne Pass, then across the Connecticut River Valley to the White Mountains.

This day was refreshingly cool, breaking the intense heat and high humidity of the pre-vious serveral weeks.

Chris and I were able to keep a steady pace

View from Eph's Lookout toward Berkshire Mountains

of three miles per hour. My diary reflects:

> "It's amazing the infinite number of
> thoughts that pass through my mind as
> I walk along-- college, home, the
> future, trees, ladies, this walk, etc.
> The rhythm of our pace is interrupted
> by the roar of an approaching stream.
> Soon the rush of water overwhelms our
> auditory sense. We turn from the surge
> of the river and once again the
> pounding of our feet and thumping of a
> noisy pack becomes the prevailing
> sound. I return to my thoughts once
> more."

We paused at Congdon Camp Cabin from 2 p.m.
to 4 p.m. and talked with a girl from Boston with
her dog. We agreed to give a flashlight and water
to a girlfriend of hers who we would meet coming
up from a store on Vermont Route 9.

Atop Harmon Hill (2,325 feet), we sat enjoy-
ing the fine panoramic view. As we gazed at all
the mountains in our midst, we wondered about the
hundreds of peaks we had already crossed in the
last 1,495 miles. We had passed trees many years
old and crossed over rocks formed millions of
years ago! They were all back along the Trail as
we had left them not able to conceive of who or
what we were about.

Saturday, July 13 we hitched a ride into
Bennington, Vermont via Route 9 where we
laundered clothes, devoured two dozen donuts, and
relaxed. Finishing our chores, we proceeded four
miles out of town to Bennington Airport to meet
Chris' father's boss, Ellis Hansen. We glided out
on his Cessna four-seater for a few days of
relaxation at his home near Mount Monadnock, N.H.
The plane ride was fabulous and I gazed out
across the wide expanse of blue sky toward the

countryside below.

Ellis' home was atop a hill overlooking the region with Mt. Monadnock prominently visible from a broad kitchen window!  Much of the house was constructed of granite and marble with a tennis court and built-in swimming pool.

We enjoyed a terrific stay - canoeing, swimming, and plenty of food.  Ellis and his wife Velta, made us feel completely welcome and, probably unknowingly, broke the tedium of our daily hiking routine.

One night was spent feasting with Ellis' and Chris' family who had come up from Swampscott, Massachusetts.  Eating dinner, we answered many questions and told interesting stories of experiences we had had on the A.T.

Reluctantly, we left the hospitable atmosphere of Ellis' home and arrived, once more, at the Trail on Route 9.  We bid Velta farewell and ten minutes later, Mother Nature welcomed us back with a downpour that completely soaked us in a matter of seconds.  I asked myself, as I had many times before, "What the hell am I doing this for?"

Walking a quick seven miles, wooden log Glastenbury Shelter lay ahead.  Several hikers were already at the lean-to including three Green Berets walking the length of the Long Trail with a group of Explorer Scouts.  Even their large, muscular frames had considerable trouble with the exerting job of walking in mountainous country. They appeared very tired.

Tuesday, July 16th mornings' walk led over a badly eroded, muddied, and overgrown trail.  My journal related:

"Passed beautiful Stratton and Bourn
Ponds.  Met a gent from New York City
wanting some advice on the skill of
backpacking and another guy from

Canada. Also passed several abandoned beaver ponds marveling at their engineering feats.

"Chris took a few good spills today on the muddy, slippery trail. At one point, he tripped and ended up doubled over with his pack still attached to his back. It made for a good laugh, at his expense. Moments later, he slipped again and fell into a patch of mud.

"Now within the vast, coniferous wilderness of the Green Mountain Range, we have left the Taconics of Connecticut and Berkshires of Massachusetts behind us. This area is beautiful but the eroded, muddy trail detracts from its true magnificence.

"Proceeding on an abandoned railway, we reached Swezey Shelter, another 20 mile day completed. We are alone at this shelter with a convenient piped spring and adjacent river for washing. The birds are singing peaceful, melodious songs at this 8 p.m. hour. Their chirping will awaken us at dawn and tell us to begin a new day."

I am certain we had scared plenty of wildlife before we got close to seeing them due to our noisy approach and scent. We had seen songbirds, squirrels, rabbits, and deer but none of the more elusive species such as black bear, bobcat, gray or red fox, or possibly mountain lion. We were, however seeing signs of beaver now.

The industrious beaver, largest of the North American rodents, can weigh upwards of 68 pounds and can measure up to 43 inches long. They range in wet, depressional areas all across America except in the extreme Southeastern and Southwestern states. They construct dams of incredible strength impounding a good deal of water. They do this to create an aquatic environment they can live in. His diet consists of bark and twigs of preferred species of poplar (aspen), willow, and cotton wood trees, and also aquatic plants. His domed house of twigs, logs, and mud with entrance and exit ways below waterline are built in the middle of these artificial lakes.

Moose are attracted to the pond area to feed on poplar and balsam fir during the winter season. As the beaver pond ages, sediments are dropped from the impounded stream creating a fertile muck. Aquatic vegetation now has a medium in which to grow providing better fish (often trout) habitat, food for moose, and a good environment for ducks and geese.

As the supply of poplars around the pond are exhausted, the beaver moves on to find a more suitable environment. So much for the interesting beaver.

Wednesday, July 17th's diary entry relates:

"Steep climb up to Bromley Mountain at elevation 3260 feet where two older women snapped pictures of us coming up the A. T. They asked questions of us, as many do. It is disheartening to reach a summit to find tourists, with instamatics, who drove their car to the top of OUR mountain.

"We proceeded through a col (an elevated mountain pass) in pretty evergreen woods and ascended steep Styles Peak (3394 feet). Traveling among majestic conifers of pine and spruce once again, the forest seemed magical. The forest floor was covered with a thick green carpet of vegeta-

112

Sign marking wet footway in Vermont

Author getting spring water at Swezey Shelter, Vt.

View toward White Mountains from the Trail

tion. These are the moments that make this adventure feel worthwhile.

"Two miles of wet, eroded trail brought us to Lost Pond Shelter. Nice guy from Springfield, Mass. here. Supper of macaroni and tomato sauce is bubbling away.

"Last night was cool and it was hell hopping out of the bag this morning. A porcupine also visited us last night but created no problem. These rodents due a considerable amount of damage in the Greens; wood of lean-tos and outhouses are often chewed up.

"After a 20.7 mile day, the problems and aggravations of the hiking day have disappeared. Bedtime draws near. I fear if I stopped during those difficult and trying moments of the day, every third word would have to be edited from this journal."

The AT was now in the 242,000 acre Green Mountain National Forest. Much of the woodland here, as in most other places along the Trail, is second growth. This region was the site of much activity during an earlier era of the pioneer and before that, the home of the American Indian.

Crossing Big Branch on an enormous suspension bridge thirty feet long and anchored by giant cement posts at either end, we reached Little Rock Pond. This is one of the most beautiful lakes in the Green Mountains where, on an island, a shelter is located according to the guidebook. Eventually we came to Clarendon Gorge on the Mill River. A washed-out suspension bridge there offered us the option of following a one mile reroute, or crossing the river. We, of course, chose the latter.

Getting half way out into the river, we

unfastened our hip belts that in the event we took a spill, we wouldn't become permanent anchors.

Suddenly we ran out of rocks to jump upon. Chris and I just barreled across the stream pell-mell putting on a hilarious display for several girls watching us from the opposite shore.

One mile later we arrived at Clarendon Shelter, a once enclosed cabin now converted to a typical AT three-sided lean-to. A fence along the front of the structure prevented cattle from wandering in from an adjoining pasture.

The next several miles led over private land in pasture, fields, and sparce woodland. Reaching Sherburne Pass, the Appalachian Trail headed east, leaving the Long Trail.

Two days after our stay at Clarendon Shelter, Chris and I both became sick; the second time I had become ill during our four months on the Trail. Our symptoms included severe fatigue, weakness, and diarrhea. We suspected water from the brook at Clarendon Shelter had been contaminated by cattle. We hiked on, nevertheless, with each step seeming like a mile. It became nearly impossible for us to move on along the Trail.

Trudging on though, we arrived eventually at Hanover, New Hampshire, with only two states left to go. Stopping to chat at the Dartmouth College Outing Club, we were directed to "frat row" to seek housing for the night. It seemed as if the entire street was lined with fraternity houses. Upon selecting one, we were invited to use the living room area as sleeping quarters. The frat's members seemed somewhat impersonal, but their offer was greatly appreciated.

On the Trail, everything was intimate and personal where talking with others was an integral part of the trail experience.

At Thayer Hall on campus, the mere price of

$3.00 bought a choice of three different dinners with four kinds of soda and three kinds of milk. Here was a chance to stuff ourselves to our heart's delight but our illness prevented it. We could only eat what little our stomachs would accept.

The next day was Sunday, July 21 and was spent recuperating from fatigue and bad diarrhea. We purchased food for the Trail and telephoned home giving no indication we were ill. Our parents already thought we were crazy for pounding ourselves over hundreds of miles of rocky trail and sleeping in the woods night after night. We lounged the day away touring Dartmouth College and the streets of Hanover, New Hampshire.

Upon picking up a package of freeze dried food and down jackets at the post office, we finally began hiking again. Katahdin in Maine was now 427 miles away!

For some time now, Chris and I were anxious to finish the Trail and return home for a much needed and well deserved rest. The Trail headed northeast out of Hanover on macadam roads for two miles and then on dirt roads, wood roads, and cut trail. The walk traversed pastures, fields, and woodland. We were now on the eastern slope of the Connecticut River Valley and the southern end of a broken range of White Mountain foothills. The A.T. was directed up to Mt. Moosilauke, southernmost peak of the Whites. Camping at Clark Pond Cabin we met through-hiker Joe Head of Connecticut. The through-hikers were now few and far between, a select group deciding not to admit to defeat but trudge on to Katahdin.

Chris and I squeeked out 28 long miles on Tuesday, July 23 along wood roads, trail, and dirt roads passable by automobile. With the exceptions of Smarts and Cube Mountains, the going was relatively level. At 7 p.m. we reached

Glencliff, N.H. where Chris was expecting mail. Rousing the postmaster, he was kind enough to get Chris' mail despite the fact that Postal Service hours were over. Pushing further along, we missed the Dartmouth Outing Club's (DOC) Great Bear Cabin, and made camp on a sloping trail.

Next morning we began the steep ascent of Mount Moosilauke (4,810 feet), a climb of 3,270 feet from Glencliff in 3.5 miles. Passing "First Water", "Last Sure Water", and thence "Go Around Rock", we reached rock cairns at tree line and glided along to the summit of Mt. Moosilauke. The majestic vistas were undescribable with the Whites lying ahead to our north.

We explored an emergency shelter held down with chains to secure it during the deadly high winds of the White Mountains. These shelters may be used in the event a sudden storm would make hiking dangerous.

The hike atop the summit was splendid with white bunchberry out in profusion in one area. A final, ridiculously steep descent of 2,300 feet in 1.4 miles rendered travelling a treacherous affair. Several ladders had to be used to descend and at times, jumping from one tree down to the next was necessary! We shared our utter disgust with the trail conditions with several poor DOC trail maintainers. Unfortunately, eroded, steep trails seemed to be the rule in the Whites.

A trail sign at the base of Moosilauke warned, "THIS TRAIL IS EXTREMELY ROUGH. IF YOU LACK EXPERIENCE, PLEASE USE ANOTHER TRAIL. TAKE SPECIAL CARE AT THE CASCADES TO AVOID TRAGIC RESULTS." No truer words could be spoken. Soon we reached Kinsman Notch at New Hampshire Highway 12.

The Appalachians of New England, of which the Whites are a component, consist of metamorphosed rock. Sediments of an ancient sea bottom were laid down during the Paleozoic Age (200-500

Chris on the open summit of Mt. Moosilauke, N.H.

million years ago). A series of tremendous geologic upheavals folded and fractured them, ultimately transforming them into marble, slate and schist.

During these geologic episodes, igneous activity injected molten rock into the existing rock formations, forming huge volcanic plugs. These plugs are typified in the granitic masses of the Presidential Range within the White Mountains. Since the Mesozoic Period (200 million years ago), erosive forces of water, wind, and chemicals, including glaciation, have been wearing these mountains down. The theory of "isostacy" again plays its role here reducing hills and mountains to an equal level with the lowlands.

It has been only 15,000 years ago, a mere instant in geologic time, that the last glacial age ended. Glacial till in the form of sand, gravel, and boulders (known as glacial erratics) was deposited in many places. The steep gorges in the Whites, known as "notches," are huge troughs cut by glacial action.

The A. T. for the next 15.5 miles led through a heavily forested region across Mt. Wolf and South Kinsman, then rapidly descending into Franconia Notch. We paused briefly there to read a lengthy description of the Appalachian Trail. Walking the length of the A.T. makes you feel the Trail is your home and was created just for you.

We moved on to Liberty Springs Campsite, 2.4 miles further. Due to the high usage of the Whites, established campsites with wooden tent platforms were provided. We argued with the caretaker that he should be honored to have two such distinguished guests in his campground and therefore, not charge us a camping fee. He had became calloused and insensitive upon dealing with hundreds of "weekend backpackers" and replied, "So what?" when I explained we were

121

walking the entire A.T. Upon that reply I lectured him on just how special the through-hiker is. I was shocked to hear such a blase attitude about the hardy end-to-ender, considering everyone we met before him was so thrilled and interested in our adventure.

We pitched our tent, <u>free of charge</u>, beside a couple from Montreal and had a pleasant talk with them. At supper that night, it was rather chilly and our down jackets were serving their purpose.

Thursday, July 26, my journal noted:

"Many steep ascents and descents today across Mts. Lincoln (5108 feet), Lafayette (5249 feet) and Garfield (4488 feet). The open summit of Mt. Lafayette offered a superb panoramic vista.

"There are two problems with White Mountains:

"1) Too many people - this entire region is accessible to too many hikers; the Trail looks like a super highway.

"2) The trails are severely eroded and in horrendous shape. Steep mountain trails need erosion control measures such as switchbacks or diversions (thank-you-maams) at specified intervals to carry water safely off the trail. The trails in the Whites are routed directly up and down the mountains perpendicular to contours; they should instead follow the contours staying on a maximum 15 - 20% grade. The steepness, though, we can handle; the rough, eroded trail is what makes hiking difficult. We travelled 12.8 miles to Galehead Hut, thought a moment, and decided to check in.

"These huts, administered by the Appalachian Mountain Club (A.M.C.), house approximately forty persons. They have large dining areas, kitchen, and mens and womens dormitories. A bed and two meals cost $12, not bad really. Hut-boys, often carrying 100 pounds, supply the huts with food and supplies where a crew prepares meals. Everyone is friendly . . .

"It's been cold and damp in the Whites; I am anxious to get to Maine."

The following morning we ate a breakfast of oatmeal, eggs and coffee at the Hut and were given a carry along lunch for the Trail. We ate that lunch shortly after leaving Galehead.

We hiked among balsam and fir, indigenous trees to the Northern Aboreal Zone. At a junction of the A.T. and Zealand Trail at 11 a.m., I mistakingly followed the latter route and walked 1.5 miles to Mt. Bond. Since the A.T. guidebook was with Chris who had taken off ahead of me earlier, I left my Kelty atop Bond and walked 3/4 miles back to Zealand Campsite. Talking with a friendly caretaker, I realized where I made my mistake. It was then 3/4 miles back to my pack and then all the way back to the A.T. Zealand Trail junction, a total of 4.5 miles out of my way!

Furious as hell, I stormed off non-stop until 4 p.m. to Crawford Notch for a grand total of 18.7 miles! And the day wasn't over yet. This was a pretty healthy mileage to cover in eight hours in the Whites with full pack! Most hikers average perhaps seven or eight miles in a day.

I shared my frustration with Chris and my anger with him for not stopping and doubling back to see if I was injured.

At the Crawford House, I picked up a package at the post office and mailed some items ahead to Rangeley, Maine.

The Crawford House is a huge building with many guestrooms and spacious lounge areas. We looked like two rag-pickers in the Waldorf-Astoria Hotel, I'm sure.

In 1792, the Crawford family of Abel, Hannah, and two sons, Ethan Allen and Erastus settled here. The soil they farmed is known as Colton fine sandy loam. This soil occupies areas on the terraces of the Saco River, at one time the flood plain of that river. The surface layer to a depth of 8 inches is a sandy loam and supplies a fair amount of water for plant growth. Further below, the sand and gravel content increases, and, hence, water percolates down rapidly. The parent material of Colton soils is largely granitic gravel. It is an important soil to farming since it is on level land with no stones in the plow layer.

Back to the Crawfords. The homestead was on a principal route through the White Mountains, so Abel decided to try the hotel business. During the next thirty years, he and his sons built inns and blazed trails so that people might enjoy the region.

Across the street from the Crawford House Inn lies a trail with a sign noting, "Crawford Path - the Oldest Continuously Used Mountain Trail Used in America. In 1819 Abel Crawford and his son Ethan Allen cleared this path to tree line near the top of Mt. Clinton. Countless thousands have travelled this path to the Presidential Range and Mt. Washington."

Chris and I ate supper at the Depot on Route 302 in Crawford Notch and called home. It

Mount Lafayette in the White Mountains

was really nice talking to my family. I missed them and my dog immensely. Mom was still keeping a diligent account of my path on her road maps.

We decided to walk the historic Crawford Path and camped a mile or so up the slope. Level ground was, indeed, difficult to find in the Whites.

On Saturday, July 27, we reached Mt. Clinton (4310 feet), a climb of 3083 feet from Crawford Notch. From the summit of Clinton, the route of the A.T. for the next thirteen miles was above tree line. Although magnificent views can be afforded there, the open ridge is exposed to the full force of all storms. It was a slightly overcast day. A yellow U.S. Forest Service sign boldly warned, "STOP - THE AREA AHEAD HAS THE WORST WEATHER IN AMERICA. MANY HAVE DIED THERE FROM EXPOSURE, EVEN IN SUMMER. TURN BACK NOW IF THE WEATHER IS BAD."

The guidebook further warned, "These storms can rise with great rapidity and incredible violence, producing winds of hurricane force and freezing conditions, even in summer. All climbers should carry ample extra clothing, and if experiencing difficulty from weather, descend to shelter by the shortest route."

Not much after I snapped a shot of the Forest Service sign, a dense fog rolled in and a light, cold drizzle began to fall. Visibility was probably not more than twenty feet. Chris and I stopped to put on heavier clothing and rain parkas and fitted rain covers to our packs. We half-heartedly convinced ourselves that our top physical condition would make it easier to scramble off the open ridge into trees in the event the bad weather intensified.

Although now in much glorified, "Presidential Range" the fog and drizzle negated any good views. Crossing Mts. Franklin and Monroe, we arrived at A.M.C. Lake-of-the-Clouds Hut. Drinking coffee, we read the trail register for several years back.

The weather report indicated no seriously bad weather. Hiking on, we passed Lake-of-Clouds, a small pond in a depression holding surface runoff and possibly underground water. The topography was such that water was ponded here, outletting into a small brook.

Arriving at the summit of Mt. Washington, we visited the tourist trap. A gift shop sold trinkets and tourists arrived by the trainload, literally, via the Cog Railroad.

Mt. Washington stands at 6288 feet, highest point in New England, with a comparable climate to Labrador, Canada, 600 miles to the north. The Indians called the mountain "Waumbekert Methna," or home of the great spirit. They never climbed it.

In the period that man has recorded weather atop Mt. Washington (since 1874), the temperature has never risen above 71 degrees Fahrenheit and has plummeted to a chilly minus 47 degrees Fahrenheit in January of 1934. Major snowfalls last into July with 178 inches of snow falling annually, at times even in the summer.

It is the wind that gives Mt. Washington the claim of having the world's worst weather. Velocities of over 75 miles per hour (hurricane force) occur about 104 days a year; winds of 100 miles per hour commonly blow during the winter season and are not uncommon in the summer months. The highest wind ever recorded by man, 231 miles per hour, was recorded in what is now an observatory; a large sign commemorates this mind boggling event.

Huge chains anchor the building down to the ground. The combination of high winds and below zero temperatures create a deadly wind-chill factor nowhere else experienced on the planet.

The severity of Mt. Washington's weather is

**STOP**

THE AREA AHEAD HAS THE WORST WEATHER IN AMERICA. EVEN IN THE

SUMMER. TURN BACK NOW IF THE WEATHER IS BAD

MANY HAVE DIED THERE FROM EXPOSURE. EVEN IN THE

**WHITE MOUNTAIN NATIONAL FOREST**

Forest Service sign in the Whites

Chris tries to find AT in dense fog

caused primarily by its location at the junction of major storm tracks. But topography also has a play in the notoriously high winds. A phenomenon known as the Bernoulli effect, causes large masses of air moving toward the summit to become compressed and accelerate as they blow up the slopes.

Fog is present 60% of the year, often limiting hiker visibility to the next trail cairn. On occasions, a dangerous "whiteout condition" occurs making it impossible to see ones own feet!

When Washington is in clear skies, it has been said one can see clear east to the Atlantic Ocean. On this foggy July day of 40 degrees Fahrenheit, this would not be the case.

The A.T. traversed the rest of the Presidentials, Mts. Jefferson, Adams, and Madison. The soil here mapped by the U.S.D.A. is rock outcrop described as, "steep rock cliffs, bare rock mountain peaks, and the high rough crest of the White Mountains. For the most part, timber line is coincidental with climatic conditions, but in some places it is at a lower elevation because of the absence of soil to support a growth of timber. Rock outcrop, as mapped, in some places includes sparcely timbered areas and in other areas supporting stunted trees that have no commercial value. Most of the rock outcrop is included in the White Mountain National Forest area. . . developed as a recreational area and crossed by numerous foot trails."

Another soil common to the Whites, at somewhat lower elevations, is mapped by the U.S.D.A. Grafton County and Coos County Soil Surveys as rough mountainous land (Herman soil material). It is described as,

> "consisting of massive land areas in
> the White Mountains cut by steep-
> walled narrow valleys and rising in

places from rolling uplands of 1500 to 2000 feet above sea level to an elevation of about 4500 feet, where alpine and subalpine conditions prevail. All this land is more or less inaccessible for farming operations, and it would be of little value for this use even if more favorably located. The rocks and soil material are largely granitic.

"Under forest cover, a gray layer 1/2-3 inches thick rests on a rich-brown layer, both being a sandy loam. Below this is a yellowish-brown fairly firm but friable subsoil a foot thick which grades into a pale-yellow light sandy loam. The substratum lies 18-20 inches below the surface and consists of sandy till. Roots can penetrate the substratum and drainage is good."

Mixed conifers of spruce and hemlock with some birch and maple grow below 3000 feet, while spruce and fir predominate above the 3000 foot elevation. The formation of soils and their associated geology is fascinating to this author.

Further on that Saturday we reached Pinkham Notch and rambled around Pinkham Notch Camp, headquarters for the A.M.C. Hut system. We looked through the many maps and trail guides available and later, ate supper there.

The following morning of Sunday, July 28 we hitched into Gorham, New Hampshire with a family from South Jersey. We ate at a McDonalds, wrote a few letters and laundered clothes where I met a nice looking woman from Atlanta, Georgia. We talked for quite a while.

Next day the A.T. traversed Mt. Hight, Carter Mountains, and Mt. Mariah to the Andros-

131

coggin Valley. We set camp at Peabody Brook at a point 1.3 miles past the crossing of the Androscoggin River and enjoyed a grand steak dinner.

Monday we began our trek of the 29.3 mile Mahoosuc Range, rival to the Stekoahs of North Carolina for the most strenuous, difficult section found on the entire Appalachian Trail.

It seemed like every word in the Maine AT Guidebook read, "ascend steeply." That description was true to the letter. In a little over nine miles, a trail sign indicated the Maine-New-Hampshire state line. Porcupines had gnawed away viciously at the sign! These animals are numerous in the Mahoosucs and Green Mountains as well as in other Northeastern and Western states.

The porcupine is easily identified as resembling an overgrown pin cushion. There are 30,000 quills distributed over the animal. They may weigh from ten to forty pounds and be up to forty inches long.

Although slow moving, the animal swims and climbs well. He prefers forested areas with conifers and poplars (aspen). Contrary to rumor, the porcupine cannot "shoot" his quills, nor does he attack other creatures.

When threatened, he stuffs his head inside his forelegs, arches his back, and keeps his posterior toward the attacker. He knows his undersides, having no quills, are vulnerable and maintains a center of gravity low to the ground to prevent being turned over. He also clicks his teeth and makes grumbling noises as a defensive tactic. If the attacker does not heed the warning, a painful experience may ensue. The porcupine's quills are loosely anchored and when touched will penetrate the attacker by the dozen. The barbed spears can be quite difficult to remove.

I remember seeing a hiker on the AT in Connecticut with his Irish Setter covered about the head with dozens of porcupine quills. The dog yelped as his master removed the spears one by one. Upon my question as to whether it was a good idea to remove them in that manner the owner replied, "Oh, this is the third time he's been into a porcupine and I've pulled the quills out this way before!" Most animals learn their lesson after their first encounter with the porcupine!

The creature can be a nuisance destroying timber and any wooden structure such as the lean-to or outhouse. The porcupine also has an affinity for salt. This makes the backpacker's shoulder straps and hip belt, covered with salt from perspiration, a potential feast for the animal.

Back to the Mahoosucs and hiking. My diary account for that Monday reflected:

"Much steep walking up half a mile and then steeply down again. Since it rained last night, rocks and stumps were slippery and the Trail muddied in sections. Crossed into Maine at 12 p.m., our last state and 280 miles to go - what a terrific feeling! There were several sheer cliffs of about twenty feet in height that were almost vertical and required careful hand-over-hand climbing to negotiate.

"Unfortunately because of fog, we did not enjoy the few open summits that were to have afforded vistas.

"So, the rivalry between the Stekoahs and Mahoosucs for the distinction of 'most difficult section of the A.T.' is undecided. Both areas are equally tough and are no place for out-of-shape hikers.

"At Full Goose Lean-to now with a

group of rather noisy teenagers. Also
here is a nice gent with his son who
talked of the many canoe trips they
had taken on the Minnesota and
Michigan Lakes.

"Also met a guy coming down from
Katahdin who is utterly disgusted with
the trial and tribulations of long
distance hiking.

"Katahdin is yet far away but very
close at the pace we keep. We have
walked through thirteen states and
have seen a great deal. I miss good
food, fruit, milk, etc."

At Full Goose Lean-to, we were four miles
into the last leg of the Mahoosucs, that stretch
between the Maine-New Hampshire border and
Grafton Notch at Maine Highway 26. The guidebook
warned, "With the exception of the Trail from the
Great Smoky Mountains to the Nantahala Range
(Stekoahs), this section from Gorham to Grafton
Notch is, for its length, probably the most
difficult portion of the Appalachian Trail."

Tuesday, July 30 saw us over the bare crest
of Fulling Mill Mountain on split logs to protect
the fragile alpine plants.

The open mountain summits at high elevations
exposed to frigid temperatures and fierce winds,
creates a harsh environment for living organisms.
Trees like balsam, spruce, and pine become
dwarfed. Heath plants like apland rosebay and
rhododendron battle the harsh environment as do
the flowering plants cinquefoil and diaspensia.
Other hardy plants of the elevated summits
include varieties of club moss and lichen.

The lichen is an interesting pioneer plant
that is actually a combination of fungus and
alga surviving in symbiotic harmony.

Animal life near tree line includes juncos,

Mahoosuc Gorge in the brutal Mahoosuc Range
(This is the AT here!)

white sparrows, and winter wren.

Hiking atop a high mountain summit with a cool mist blowing creates a somber, peaceful mood that is unforgetable and will beckon hikers back to the high places again and again.

From the South Peak of Fulling Mill Mountain, Chris and I descended steeply into Mahoosuc Notch. The Notch is a sheer gulch filled with boulders and has precipitous walls. For 0.93 miles, the Trail travels over boulders and through caves. The guidebooks warns that the route here is difficult and dangerous, and that care must be exercised on damp moss. Naturally, it had rained the previous night before making the wet, moss covered boulders even more treacherous.

At times we had to remove our packs to squeeze through the narrow caves. To this point in our hike, we were easily averaging three miles per hour even in steep terrain. Our time in Mahoosuc Notch however, was a humbling 1/2 mile per hour! This demanding traverse was followed by the extremely steep ascent of Mahoosuc Arm and Old Speck Mountain.

I would vote that those five miles, due to strenuous climbing and wet, treacherous footway, were the roughest we encountered on the entire AT.

We finally descended into Grafton Notch and my diary declared:

"The Mahoosucs are over and they were very, very tough. In Grafton Notch Lean-to now with a group of cyclers and I hope they're ready for bed soon. "I am very tired and it's been a long day. My knee really hurts from all those strenuous, Mahoosuc ups and downs."

Vista from Baldpate Mountain in Maine

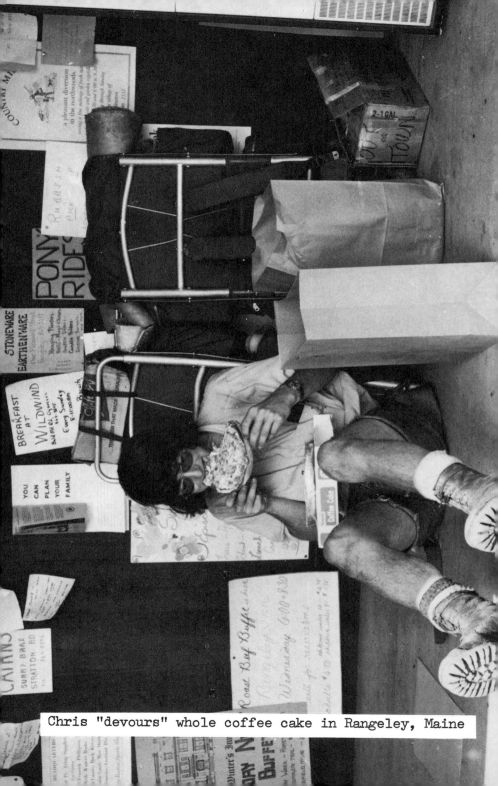

Chris "devours" whole coffee cake in Rangeley, Maine

The following day of Wednesday we traversed
the summit of 3800 foot Baldpate Mountain. It
was a bright beautiful day looking from Baldpate
with its striking panoramic views! Trail conditions past this peak were bad - mud, overgrown
trail, and eroded footway.

We passed Surplus and C ponds, and lumber
camps so characteristic of Maine in a spruce and
fir woodland. We pushed on after dinner and
hiked close to Maine Route 5 for a 20 mile day.

We awoke next morning to the sound of lum-
berjacks' chainsaws. The A.T. slabbed Elephant
Mountain through a majestic spruce forest, then
reached Maine Highway 17 where we hitched a ride
into Rangeley, Maine.

Chris and I attended to errands and returned back to our home, the A.T., by 4 p.m. Mosquitoes attacked us in droves in numbers like I'd
never seen before and got into our eyes, mouths,
and ears. Insect repellent was useless, no matter how great the dosage. Luckily, though, we
had missed the dreaded black fly season of May
through June.

Walking on lumber tote-roads, we camped a
little further on.

For the next several days, we maintained a
swift pace passing the Sugarloaf and Mt. Bigelow
Ranges. Hiking the Bigelows was very rewarding
as we passed through beautiful spruce and fir
forests.

The A.T. in Maine leads through utter wilderness in its 280 mile course. Therefore, ut-
most care must be exercised to avoid losing the
route of the Trail, for once lost, the hiker may
find himself in a serious predicament. The Maine
A.T. Guidebook said, as true on other portions of
the A.T.,

"In case of doubt as to the route,
stop. Do not go forward. Retrace

139

your route deliberately, carefully and slowly, until you return to some clear indication of the Trail. Inspection will then usually disclose the point of the initial error. The cardinal mistake and the basis for an unfortunate experience is a headlong, precipitous insistence on going forward when the route seems obscure or dubious. Haste, such as in a desire to avoid darkness or to reach camp, only precipitates the difficulty . . . It is far preferable, when in doubt, to overcome the urge to travel and remain at the point of difficulty, since this prevents straying far from the route. A night out close to the Trail is far preferable to the disability of being genuinely lost."

Advice one would do well to heed.

Passing East Carry and Pierce Ponds, we arrived at the Kennebec River. The Kennebec was utilized in floating logs down river to lumbering mills. Water flow is controlled upstream, releasing a greater volume of water when logs are in the river. The combination of rapidly rising water and huge logs can present quite a problem to the hiker since no bridge is provided there. Several individuals now ferry hikers across the Kennebec for a fee; we crossed without this aid.

It was now Friday, August 2, as we stopped at the combination general store and post office at Caratunk, Maine. This was one of only two towns the Trail passed directly through in all of Maine. We made camp just off Pleasant Pond Road.

Next day we hiked only 14 miles since we expected mail there, but could not pick it up until Monday.

Moxie Bald at 2400 feet with its granite

ledges and Arctic features was splendid. We camped at Moxie Bald Lean-to.

In my diary, I summed up some of my feelings on the journey:

"Georgia was well maintained and afforded many fine views. This was State #1 and we all had to get into condition. Many adamantly claimed there that they would walk the entire Appalachian Trail. All of us were disillusioned by what walking the Trail was all about; we couldn't foresee the boredom, frustration, and hard, hard work involved to reach Katahdin.

"The folks in the Southern states were friendly but a bit apprehensive of strangers at first. Most would assist you when asked.

"The Great Smoky Mountains and Roan Mountain Cloudland area were my favorite sections of the entire Trail.

"Maryland, Pennsylvania, New Jersey and New York were not very impressive when compared to the scenic grandeur of the 5000 and 6000 foot Southern Appalachians, but had some pretty areas as well to offer.

"Connecticut, Massachusetts and Vermont had its local charm. New Hampshire's White Mountains afforded outstanding vistas, but the campsite system and impersonalism made me glad to leave that region.

"The Northern trails can't compare to the well maintained trails of the Southern Appalachians. Maine's mosquitoes, gnats, and no-see-ums are very bothersome. Much of the land in

Maine, save for the southwestern
areas, is low lying and swampy keeping our feet constantly wet.
"Our journey nears its end. . . . "

We finally met up with through-hiker Burt
Makar of Lincoln Park, New Jersey. We had been
keeping note of Burt's progress in the trail
registers, as we had of other long distance
hikers ahead of us.

We took a refreshing swim at Bald Mountain
Pond in front of Moxie-Bald Lean-to.

We arrived in Monson, Maine on Sunday,
August 4th, and found no decent accomodations.
We checked into a rather run down room in a
private home for $4.00 a piece, the most
expensive lodging we had encountered. We took
showers, wrote several letters, and gourged
ourselves as usual, at the local store.

Letters I received from my mother and
sister had "On to Katahdin" inscribed on the
envelopes.

Out of Monson we followed 2 miles of dirt
and paved roads and eventually reached Bodfish
Farm, where a 100 year old farmhouse still stood.

Traversing the Barren-Chairback Range we
reached Barren Mountain Firetower (2670 feet). A
magnificent panorama swept out across Maine's
vast, unbroken wilderness and ponds and lakes
dotted the landscape.

The guidebook noted, "Prior to lumbering in
1939 by the St. Regis Paper Company, the Barren-
Chairback Range with its five peaks was an unbroken coniferous forest. It was characterized
by the somber, cathedral-like aspect of its ever-
greens with deep patches of caribou and sphagnum
moss." The A.T. now follows some of the old lumber haul roads.

A 1/4 mile blue blazed trail led to our
camp for the night, Cloud Pond Lean-to, situated

Pond in the scenic Bigelow Range of Maine

Sunlit Appalachian Trail, Maine

AT leads <u>through</u> beaver pond in Maine lowlands

in a pristine setting against Cloud Pond. It had
been a long 28 mile day in addition to getting
lost for a few hours. A troublesome wisdom tooth
was also acting up that night.

We had noted moose tracks frequently now.
The following day, Tuesday, August 6th, we hiked
another 21 mile day past Chairback Mountain
Sporting Camps. A number of these camps are
located on Maine lakes accessible by plane or
rough terrain vehicles.

We had bid farewell to Burt Makar at White
Brook Lean-to; he was to finish at Katahdin in 5
days, we in 4 days.

We talked with French-Canadian lumbermen on
a lumber road which also served as the Trail. We
then forded beautiful Pleasant River with boots
on to avoid slipping on rocks.

The insects had been wild - mosquitoes at
night and black gnats by day.

An interesting diary entry on Wednesday,
August 7, relates:

> "Began hiking at 7:15 a.m. after a
> nasty breakfast with mosquitoes. We
> paused for a snack and picture taking
> at 9:45 a.m. when Chris exclaimed,
> 'There's a moose heading down the
> trail!' We gave chase about 50 feet
> behind her, as the forest floor shook
> from her weight. She wouldn't stop
> for a portrait though, she was huge!"

The moose is the largest antlered animal in
the world and tallest mammal in the Americas. A
large bull moose can stand more than six and one
half feet at the shoulders and be up to ten and
one half feet long. It may weigh upwards of 1800
pounds. Moose are found in Maine, several Western states, and in most regions of Canada.

Further along that same day, a beaver had

constructed a pond in the middle of the
Appalachian Trail and we found ourselves walking
through one foot of water.

The walking was level, but the Trail was
often muddied and overgrown.

We ended our 22.8 mile day at abandoned
Antlers Camp at Lower Jo-Mary Lake where cabins
with useable bunks and stoves still remained.
After taking a swim, we ate dinner.

That night proved to be the most miserable
night of our trip. The cabin was hot and full of
mosquitoes. Pitching our tent outside we hoped
for relief, but tiny no-see-ums penetrated the
tent and ate us alive. Our only recourse was to
bury ourselves in our sleeping bags and roast on
that hot, humid night!

Next morning we awoke early at 5:30 a.m. in
hopes of leaving the bugs behind. I then fully
appreciated the stories of people going mad from
annoying inscects in these Maine woods!

Passing Pemadumcook and Nahmakanta Lakes, we
ate lunch at "Sand Beach" on Nahmakanta.

Proceeding ahead that Thursday, we had
arrived at Rainbow Lake and looked to our left to
see Mount Katahdin! It rose majestically into the
sky some 5,267 feet up; its' grandeur commanding
our entire view.

Pausing briefly for supper, we moved on
until 8 p.m., our final goal now within sight.
After a 28 mile day, we camped on an open summit
of an unnamed peak to witness the most
extraordinary sunset of our trip. It was a
beautiful night with a cool breeze, no bugs, a
great sunset, and Katahdin only 20 miles away.

My Friday night, August 9 journal entry
read:

"Today was a good day. Last night, a
million stars shone brightly in the
black Maine sky as the streaks of the

147

Our first view of Mt. Katahdin from Rainbow Lake

Milky Way were clearly visible. It was a night to reflect on our long journey and gaze at the stars, but sleep came quickly.

"Awaking at 5:30 a.m. this morning, Katahdin was crisply outlined by a red sky still hiding the morning sun. I hopped out of my sleeping bag in a cool 30 degrees and set up my camera and tripod. The sun then brilliantly rose over the eastern sky beginning our last day of walking with a pack. That sunrise cannot be adequately described in words; my solemn mood, Katahdin in the near distance, and the red glow of the sun making its way over the hills created a feeling that is all mine.

"Chris arose and we picked a mountain delicacy - blueberries, and then ate breakfast.

"We got wet at Abol Stream (no bridge) and then walked beside Nesowadnehunk Stream with its gigantic boulders and violently raging waters. Passing Daicey Pond, we then reached Katahdin Stream Campground, in Baxter State Park for a 14.6 mile day. After being told there was no room left in the campground, we were fuming. After 2045 miles from Georgia, they didn't have room for us! A friendly ranger gave us a lift 2 miles back to Daicey Pond near twin Lean-tos.

"The trip is essentially over now - only 5.2 miles more to Baxter Peak atop Katahdin. The adventure now seems worth it. . ."

The next morning, Saturday, we caught a

149

2000-miler Chris at Hunt Spur atop Katahdin

Only "1 mile" left to Trail's end

ride back to Katahdin Stream Campground to begin our ascent of Baxter Peak, a climb of 4156 feet in five miles.

Katahdin, "greatest mount" to the Indians, is an immense granite monolith 5267 feet high, the highest point in Maine. According to geologists, a hot molten mass of granite rose towards the surface of the ground, then thrusting itself finally a mile into the sky. We took our first step - toward our final goal at 9 a.m. Emerging from the timber, we ascended Hunt Spur around and over massive granite boulders. Careful foot placement was imperative. Several difficult areas were provided with iron hand holds anchored in the rock to hoist oneself up.

We moved expediously; Baxter Peak, "1 mile," was painted on a rock. A final surge and we reached Katahdin, northern terminus of the Appalachian Trail! I gave a yell, throwing my canteen in the air in a burst of joy! Finally, we had reached our goal - a mountain peak in north central Maine, 2050 miles and fourteen states from Springer Mountain, Georgia. The feeling of accomplishment and excitement were none like I had ever felt before! Katahdin - Saturday, August 10, 10:53 a.m.

We eventually calmed down and then sat solemnly, gazing across the vast expanse of Maine, a view unobstructed on all sides. There were no more mountains ahead of us - the white 2 x 6 blazes led north no longer. . . .

We had reached Katahdin in an especially fast time - 1 hour and 53 minutes, most hikers require about 4 hours.

We had taken plenty of photos at the trail sign stating, "Baxter Peak, Northern Terminus of the Appalachian Trail." News of the completion of our hike travelled quickly among the other hikers atop Katahdin. They all asked questions and wanted to know more of our accomplishment. Se-

Chris Wile and Don Fortunato(right) at Mt. Katahdin,
northern terminus of the Appalachian Trail

veral asked, "Where do you go from here?" Smiling we replied, "Hell, go home and relax!"

Chris and I left Katahdin at half past noon on a crystal clear Maine day with deep blue skies. We hitchhiked into Lake Millinocket, Maine and called a friend of Chris', John McDevitt. He had a summer cabin on Millinocket and fed us and put us up for the night.

Ellis Hansen once again flew us by plane to Chris' home in Swampscott, Massachusetts on Sunday, August 11. His family was very happy to see us and I spent the next two days relaxing and reflecting on our journey.

I wrote that for the previous four months we had endured sweat, mud, rough trail, rain, and wet feet, but that we had seen the most scenic mountain country in Eastern America and met interesting people along the way.

The intense effort and perserverance we exhibited had finally paid off. We had completed the Appalachian Trail in a single season; an accomplishment only a handful can claim. I realized there is a great reward in accepting a grueling challenge and then being able to claim victory by completing your goal. This idea came clearly into focus when I read the trail sign, "Katahdin."

I would most surely recommend to prospective 2,000 milers a slower, more relaxed pace than we had kept. An average of fifteen miles per day gives the hiker more time to enjoy the Trail, relax more in camp, or perhaps fish in the numerous streams along the way. Hiking the Appalachian Trail is certainly enough work without trying to meet a rigorous schedule of twenty to twenty five miles a day.

It was time to say goodbye to my friend and partner, Chris Wile, and head home. We landed at Morristown Airport in Hansen's plane and met my family there. It was good to see them and my

154

friends again.

My journey on the Appalachian Trail had come to an end. It was a personal achievement I will always be proud of and an adventure I will never forget.

## REFERENCES

Brooks, Maurice. The Appalachians.
Houghton-Mifflin Co., Boston, Mass. 1965.

Caras, Roger A. North American Mammals.
Meredith Press, N.Y., 1967.

Fisher, Ronald M. The Appalachian Trail.
National Geographic Society, Washington,
D.C., 1972.

Fletcher, Colin. The Thousand Mile Summer.
Howell-North Books, Berkeley, Calif., 1964.

Garvey, Edward B. Appalachian Hiker II.
Appalachian Books, Oakton, Va., 1971.

Gilluly, James; Waters, Aaron; and Woodford, A.O.
Principles of Geology Third Edition.
Freeman and Co., San Francisco, 1968.

Hutchins, Ross E. Plants Without Leaves.
Dodd, Mead & Company, N.Y., 1966.

Leet, Don L. and Judson, Sheldon. Physical
Geology Fourth Edition. Prentice-Hall,
Inc., Englewood Cliffs, N.J., 1971.

New York-New Jersey Trail Conference. New York
Walk Book. Doubleday/Natural History Press,
Garden City, N.Y., 1971.

Engineering Field Manual, U. S. D. A. Soil
Conservation Service. Chapter 12 - Spring
and Wells, compiled by Daniel Griswold.

United States Department of Agriculture, Soil Conservation Service, Soil Survey of:

- Sevier County, Tennessee, August 1956.

- Cocke County, Tennessee, March, 1955

- Sussex County, New Jersey, August 1975.

- Grafton County, New Hampshire, April, 1939.

- Coos County, New Hampshire, August. 1943.